TRADING CHART PATTERNS

Yogesh Rohitwal

1st Edition: Dec 2023

ISBN: 9798871584064

Self Published

Written by Yogesh Rohitwal

Disclaimer

The information in this book is meant to teach people about stock research and help them get better at it.

I have tried to stay away from giving my opinion on any stock in this book as much as possible, but if I did, it is only for teaching purposes. It is not a suggestion to buy, sell, or hold something.

If someone reads this book and then invests or trades in the financial markets and loses money because of a mistake, an inability, or anything else, the author, publisher, printer, composer, and/or seller are not responsible, either individually or together.

Each person should trade or buy in financial market instruments based on his or her own knowledge, understanding, and common sense, as well as a proper and logical analysis of the market situation and a good reading of the market.

I used charts from the Tradingview.com

Content

Support and Resistance

Support and resistance are basic ideas that help investors find their way in the fast-paced world of stock trading. Support can be thought of as a price floor that a stock tends to find stable and not want to fall below.

On the other hand, resistance is like a price ceiling; it's a level that stocks often have a hard time breaking through. These levels are not made up; they are based on how the market has behaved in the past.

Support and resistance are important parts of technical analysis because they help traders guess how prices might move. When a stock gets close to support, it might be a good time to buy, and when it gets close to resistance, it might be a good time to sell.

Investors can make better decisions, set stop-loss orders, or find entry and exit points when they know these levels. By understanding and using these ideas, traders can get a big advantage in the stock market, which is very unpredictable.

What does "support" mean?

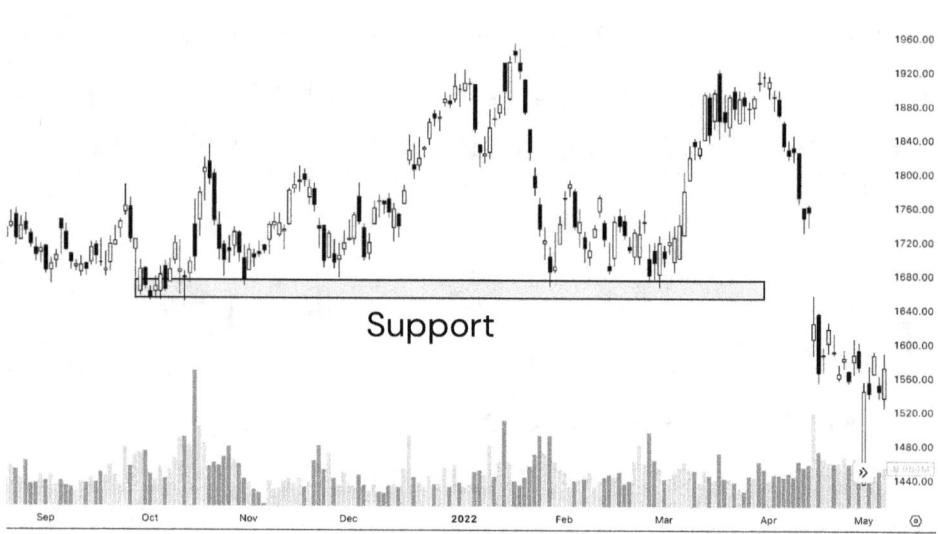

As the name suggests, it's the point where the price of a security stops falling because there's enough demand to keep it from going down any further.

As we've already talked about, the price of a security goes down when quantity is higher than demand. Now, as the price gets closer to the support level, more and more people want to buy the security. This means that demand is higher than supply, so the price stops falling and begins to go up.

There will always be support below a security's current market price.

Support level or zone gives us a point of reference for where the most repeated buying (demand) has happened in the past and is likely to happen again in the future. From the point of view of market participants, it's an important trading level.

What does "resistance" mean?

As the name suggests, it is the point where the price of security stops going up because there is enough supply to keep it from going up anymore.

As was already said, the price of a security goes up when demand is higher than supply. Now, as the price gets closer to the resistance level, more and more people want to sell the security. This means that there are more sellers than buyers, so the price stops going up and starts going down.

Resistance will always show up above a security's current market price.

The resistance level or zone tells us where selling (supply) has happened the most often in the past and is likely to happen again in the future. From the point of view of people who trade on the market, it is an important level.

Candlestick Patterns

Candlestick Patterns are patterns made by a single candle or by putting two or more candles together in a certain order. Such patterns help a trader look at how the price of an asset has moved in the past and how it is moving now to spot reversals or continuations of a trend. Traders use these patterns to find trading chances.

Candlestick patterns show what buyers and traders are doing, which is why they are important to study.

Before we go any further, let's first look at how candles are made.

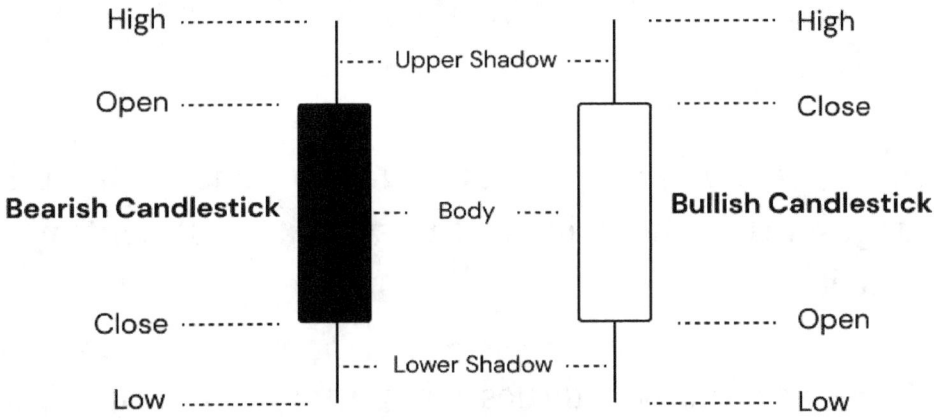

As the picture shows, a candle shows the high, low, opening, and closing prices of an asset for a certain period.

There are two kinds of candles: bullish and bearish.

Bullish Candle -

A candle is called "bullish" when the close price is higher than the open price. The body of this kind of candle is such as white or green.

This candle shows that people are optimistic and that the price of the asset is likely to go up even more.

Bearish Candle -

When the close price is lower than the open price, a candle is referred to as bearish. This candle's body is black or red.

Such a candle represents negative sentiment and suggests that the price of the security will continue to decline.

There are many candlestick patterns, but in this book, I will explain the most common ones that give very good results and are often seen on charts.

Hammer

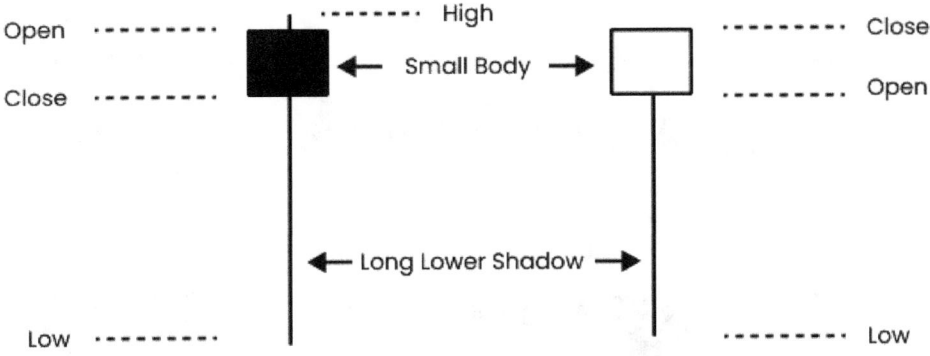

The Hammer pattern is a bullish candlestick pattern that can indicate a potential reversal in a downtrend. It forms when the price opens near its low, rallies significantly during the session, and closes near its open. The candlestick resembles a hammer, with a small body and a long lower shadow.

This pattern suggests that buyers are stepping in and pushing the price higher, signaling a potential shift in market sentiment. Traders often use the hammer pattern as a buying signal, anticipating a bullish move in the future.

Inverted Hammer

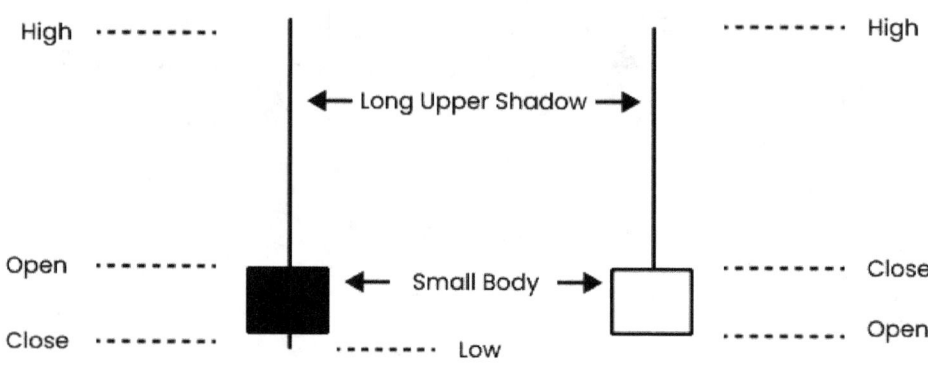

This pattern is the inverse of the hammer pattern. It is a bullish reversal candlestick pattern. A candle with a small body, little or no lower shadow, and a long upper shadow forms this pattern at the bottom of a downtrend.

Normally, the upper shadow in this pattern should be at least twice the size of the real body. The real body can be either red (black) or green (white). However, an inverted hammer with a green (white) real body gives a stronger bullish signal.

Bullish Engulfing

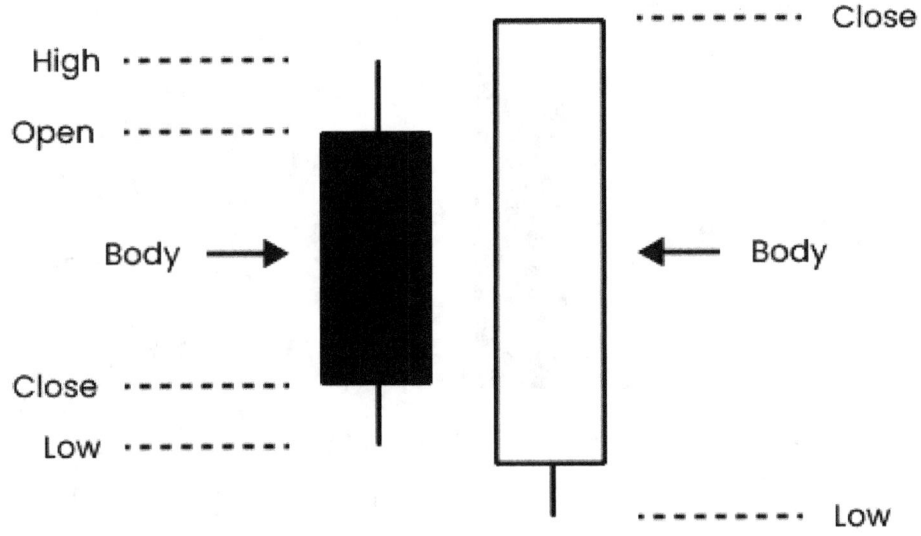

The bullish engulfing pattern is a candlestick pattern that indicates a potential reversal in a downtrend. It consists of two candles, where the first candle is a smaller bearish candle and the second candle is a larger bullish candle that completely engulfs the first candle.

This pattern suggests that buyers have overwhelmed sellers, leading to a shift in momentum and a possible upward trend. Traders often look for confirmation signals before making trading decisions.

Piercing Line

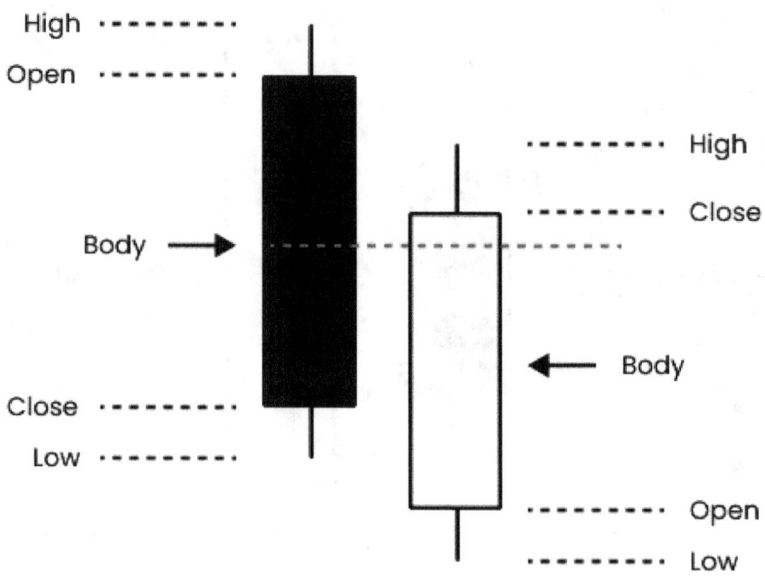

The piercing line pattern is a bullish reversal pattern that occurs during a downtrend. It consists of two candlesticks: the first is a long red (black) candle, followed by a long green (white) candle that opens below the low of the previous candle but closes above its midpoint.

This pattern suggests a shift in sentiment from bearish to bullish and indicates potential upward momentum in the market. Traders often consider it a signal to enter long positions or to close out short positions.

Morning Star

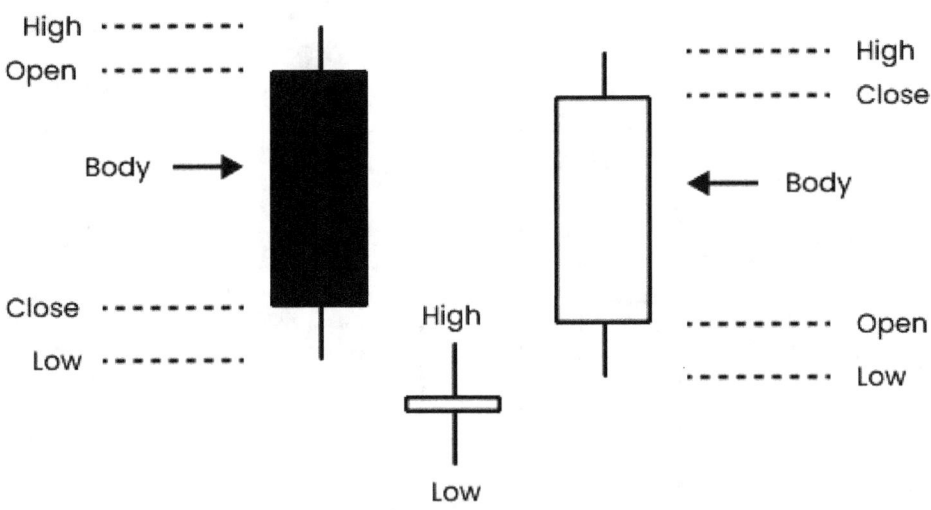

The Morning Star pattern is a bullish candlestick pattern that signals a potential reversal in a downtrend. It consists of three candles: a long bearish candle, followed by a small-bodied candle (either bullish or bearish) that gaps below the first candle, and finally a strong bullish candle that closes above the midpoint of the first candle.

This pattern suggests that the bears are losing control and the bulls may take charge, leading to a potential upward movement in price. It is considered a reliable pattern when it occurs after a significant downtrend.

Three White Soldiers

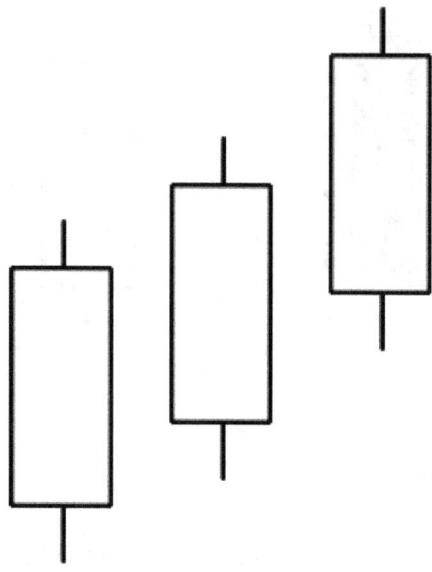

The Three White Soldiers pattern is a bullish reversal pattern that consists of three consecutive long green (or white) candlesticks, with each candlestick closing higher than the previous one. This pattern suggests strong buying pressure and indicates a potential reversal of a downtrend.

It signifies a shift in market sentiment from bearish to bullish. Traders often interpret this pattern as a signal to enter long positions or as an indication of a continued upward trend.

Bullish Marubozu

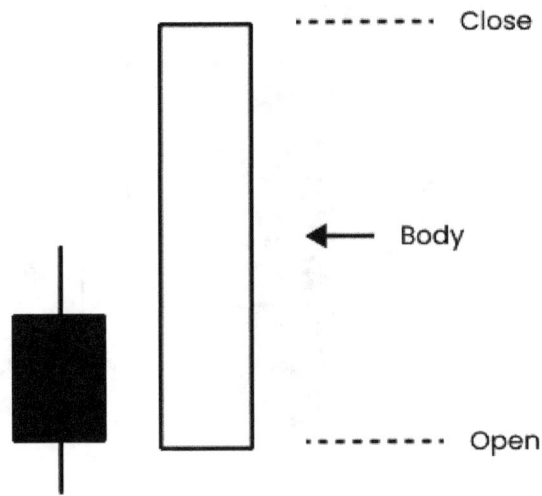

The bullish marubozu candlestick pattern is a strong bullish candlestick pattern that indicates the continuation of an upward trend. It has a long body with no upper and lower shadows. The opening price is usually near the candle's low, and the closing price is near the high.

This pattern suggests that buyers dominated the market throughout the trading session, indicating strong bullish sentiment. Traders frequently interpret the bullish marubozu as a sign of sustained buying pressure and may interpret it as a signal to enter long positions or hold existing bullish positions.

Bullish Harami

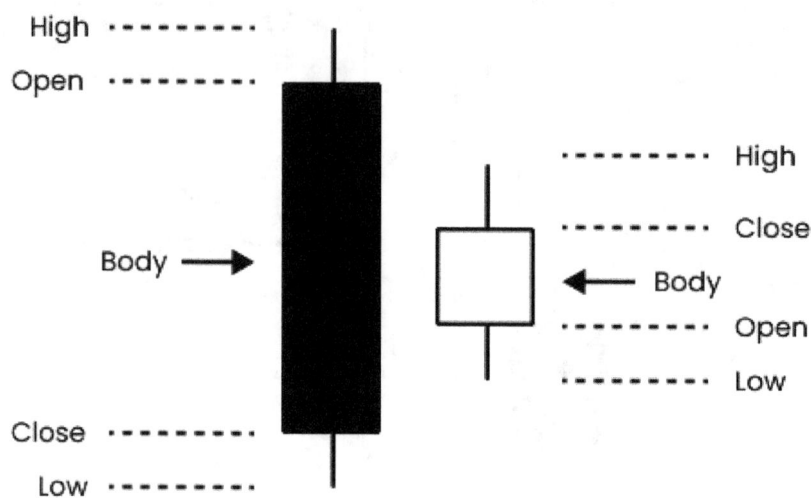

Bullish Harami is a bullish reversal pattern that appears during a downward trend. The pattern gets its name from the Japanese word harami, which means "pregnant woman," due to the graphic representation's resemblance to a pregnant woman.

During a downtrend, the first candle in this pattern is typically a large red (black) bearish candle, followed by a small green (white) bullish candle with a small body and comparatively smaller lower and upper shadows. The body of the second candle is within the body of the previous candle.

Tweezer Bottom

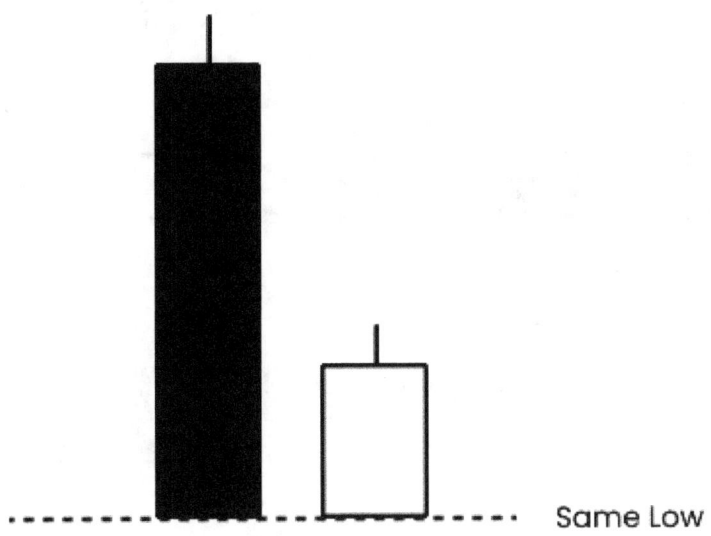

Same Low

The tweezer bottom pattern is a bullish candlestick pattern that occurs at the bottom of a downtrend. It consists of two candlesticks with the same low price level, resembling a pair of tweezers. The first candlestick is typically a bearish candle, indicating selling pressure. The second candlestick is a bullish candle, signaling a potential reversal in the downtrend.

This pattern suggests that buyers are stepping in to support the price, which may lead to a bullish trend reversal. Traders often interpret the tweezer bottom pattern as a buying opportunity.

Hanging Man

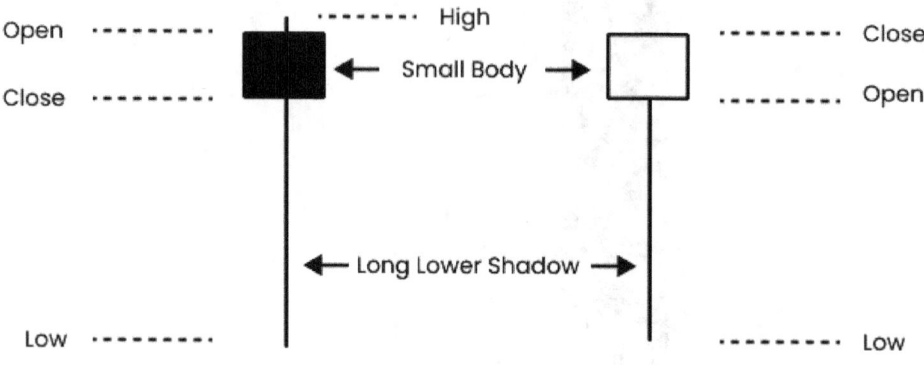

The Hanging Man pattern is a bearish candlestick pattern that occurs at the top of an uptrend. It consists of a single candlestick with a small body and a long lower shadow, resembling a hanging man.

The pattern suggests that sellers are gaining control, as the price opened high but closed near the low. It indicates a potential reversal in the uptrend and may lead to a bearish trend. Traders often view this pattern as a selling opportunity.

Shooting Star

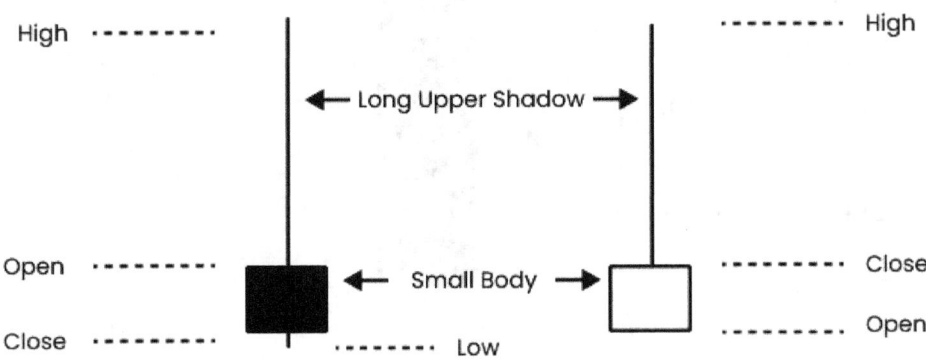

The shooting star is a bearish candlestick pattern that suggests prices may be approaching a top. It is characterized by a small real body and a long upper shadow.

This pattern indicates that buyers initially pushed the price higher but were overpowered by sellers, resulting in a potential reversal in the uptrend. The long upper shadow represents the rejection of higher prices and is seen as a selling opportunity.

Bearish Engulfing

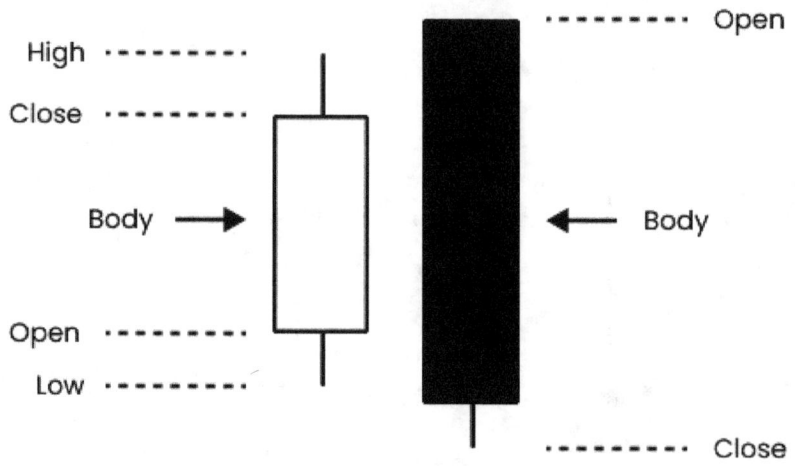

The Bearish Engulfing pattern is a bearish reversal pattern that occurs at the top of an uptrend. It consists of two candlesticks: the first is a smaller bullish candle, and the second is a larger bearish candle. The bearish candle engulfs the bullish candle, indicating a change in sentiment from bullish to bearish.

Traders can sell using this pattern by selling at the close of the second candle, waiting until the next candle to sell to verify the pattern, or waiting for other signals such as a price break below support. The larger the bearish candle compared to the bullish candle, the stronger the bearish sentiment.

Evening Star

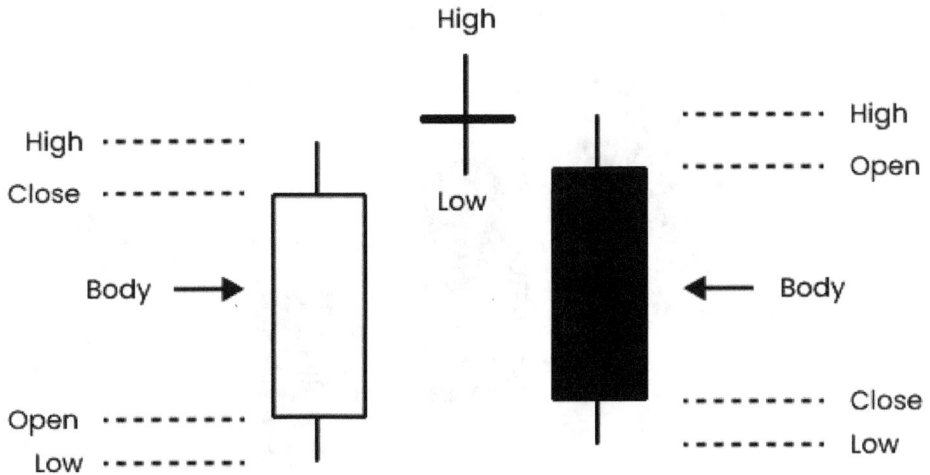

The Evening Star pattern is a bearish reversal pattern that consists of three candles. It typically appears after an uptrend and signals a potential trend reversal to the downside. The first candle is a large bullish candle, followed by a small-bodied candle (either bullish or bearish) that gaps up or down from the first candle. The third candle is a larger bearish candle that closes below the midpoint of the first candle.

This pattern suggests a weakening of bullish momentum and indicates a possible trend reversal, making it important for traders to consider selling positions or taking short positions.

Three Black Crows

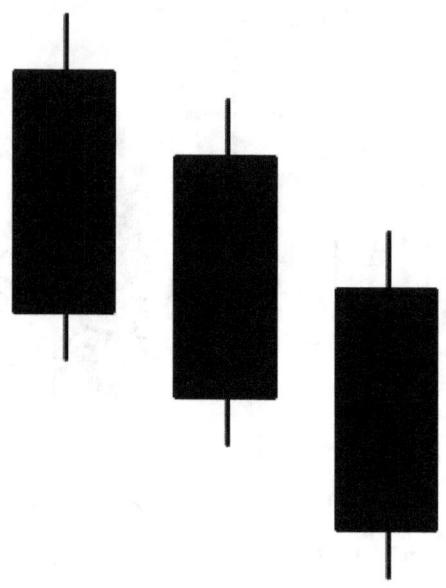

The Three Black Crows pattern is a bearish reversal pattern that occurs in an uptrend. It consists of three consecutive long-bodied bearish candlesticks with lower lows and lower highs. Each candlestick opens within the previous candle's body and closes near its low.

This pattern suggests a strong shift in sentiment from bullish to bearish and indicates that sellers have taken control. Traders often interpret it as a signal to sell or take profits, as it suggests the potential for a trend reversal to the downside.

Dark Cloud Cover

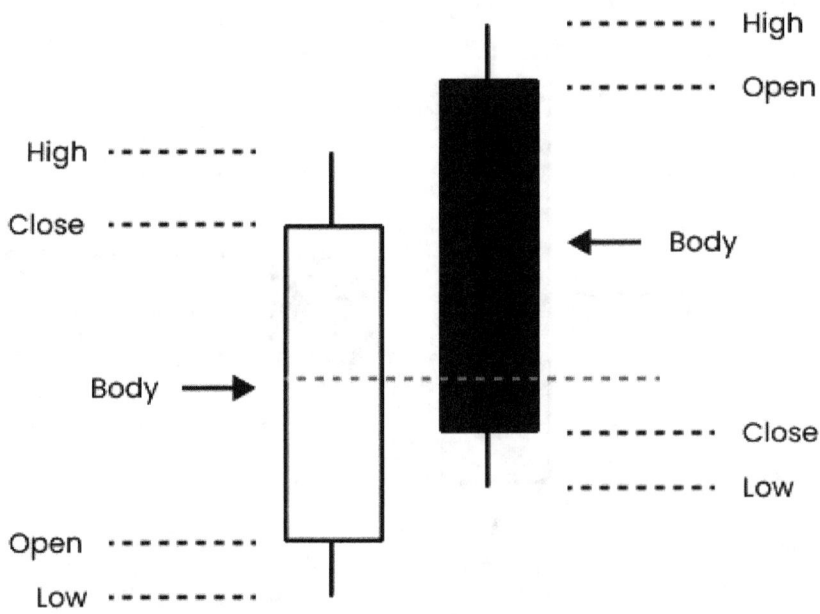

The Dark Cloud Cover pattern is a bearish reversal candlestick pattern. It occurs when a bearish candle closes below the middle of the previous candle. This pattern suggests a potential reversal to a downward trend.

However, it is important to note that the dark cloud cover has a poor reversal performance, with only a 60% chance of a reversal occurring. Traders should wait for confirmation from other indicators before making any trading decisions.

Bearish Harami

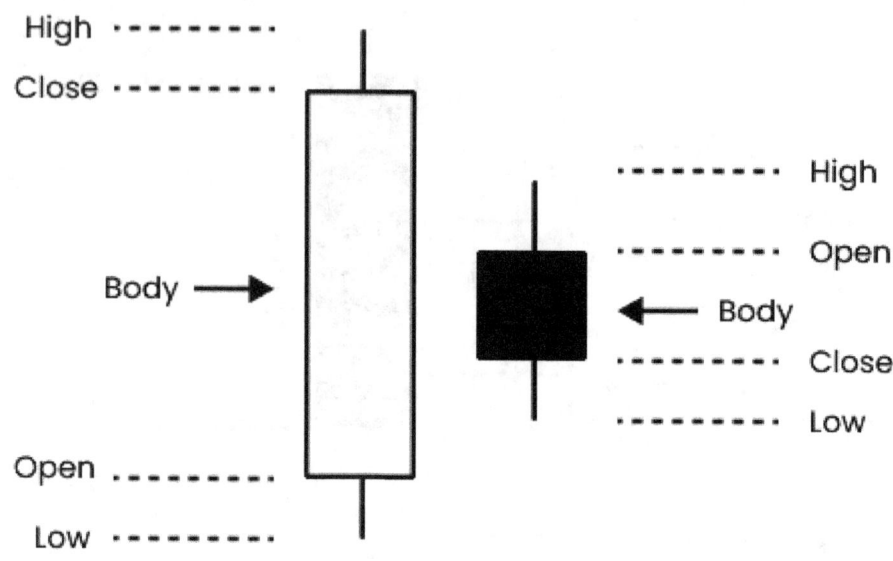

The Bearish Harami pattern is a two candlestick reversal pattern that occurs in an uptrending market. It consists of a small red (black) real body candlestick, followed by a smaller green (white) real body candlestick that is completely engulfed by the body of the previous.

This pattern suggests a potential trend reversal from bullish to bearish. However, traders question the reliability of this pattern as a reversal indicator, and it is advisable to consider other indicators and patterns for confirmation.

Tweezer Top

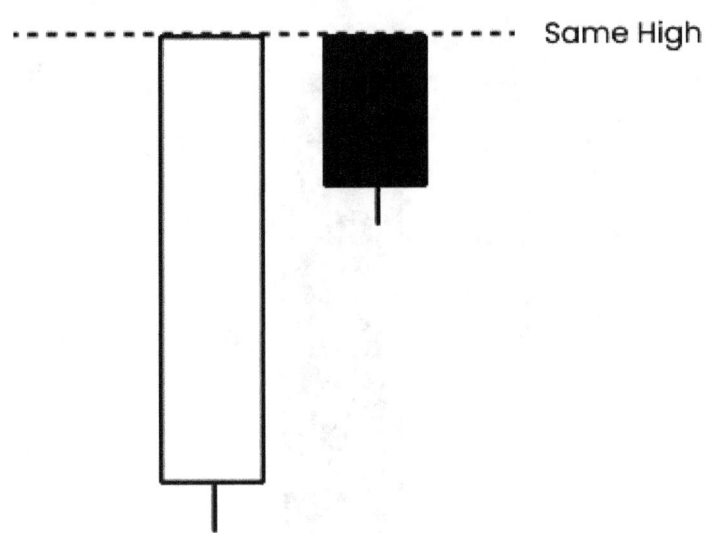

Same High

Traders often observe the Tweezer Top pattern as a bearish reversal pattern occurring at the top of uptrends. It consists of two candlesticks with the same matching tops, usually composed of shadows. It occurs when buyers push prices higher but are unable to push the top any further.

The Tweezer Top signals a market top and signifies an area of resistance. If the Tweezer Top appears at market highs, has a large first candle and a short second candle, or is followed by another reversal pattern, it is considered more reliable.

Bearish Marubozu

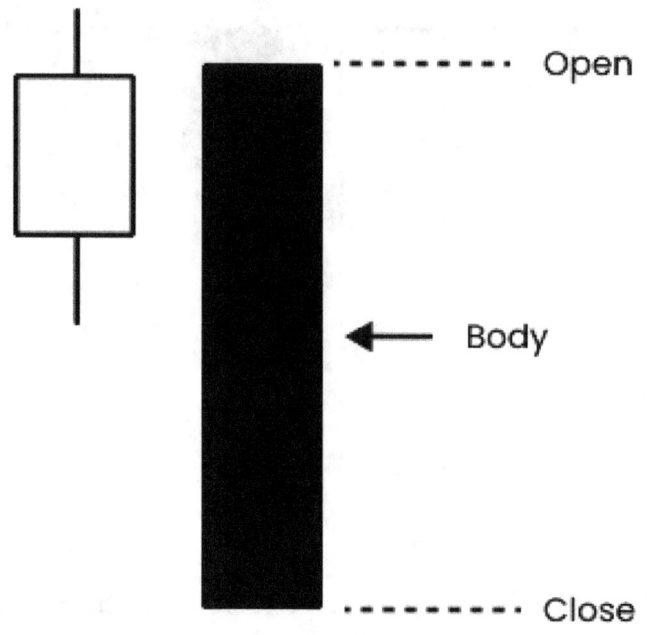

The bearish marubozu pattern is a strong bearish reversal candlestick pattern. It occurs when the open price is the highest point of the session and the closing price is the lowest point, with no upper or lower shadows. This indicates intense selling pressure throughout the entire session.

The pattern suggests that bears are in complete control and that the price may continue to decline. Traders often interpret this pattern as a sign of a potential trend reversal from bullish to bearish.

Doji

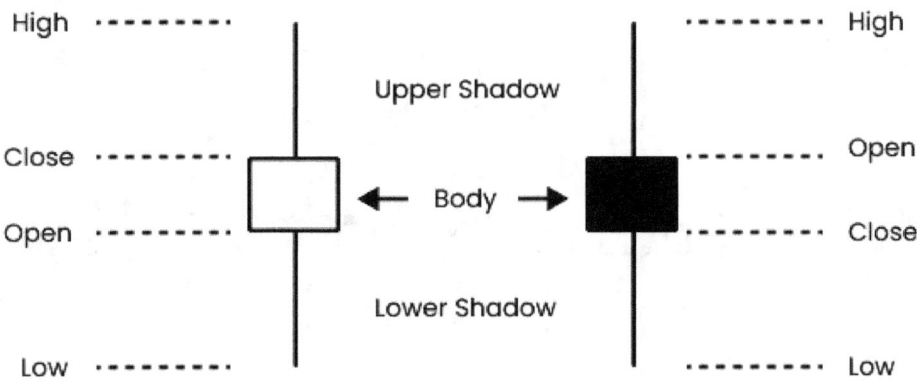

A Doji pattern is a candlestick formation that indicates indecision between buyers and sellers in the market. It occurs when the opening and closing prices are almost identical, creating a small-bodied candlestick with long shadows. This pattern suggests a possible trend reversal or continuation.

However, it is important to use it in conjunction with other analysis tools for confirmation. There are different types of Doji patterns, including the neutral, long-legged, dragonfly, gravestone, and four-priced Doji, each with its own implications for market trends and potential reversals.

Long-Legged Doji

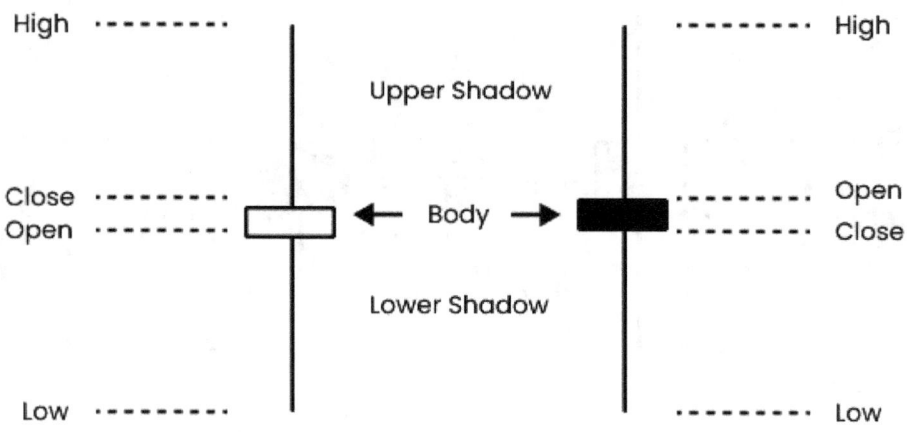

The long-legged doji is a candlestick pattern that signals market indecision. It has long upper and lower shadows and a small real body in the center. This pattern suggests a potential price reversal or continued price volatility. It is most significant after a strong advance or decline and can mark the start of a consolidation period or trend reversal.

Traders can trade the pattern by waiting for the price to move above or below the long-legged doji or by waiting for a consolidation to form around it.

Spinning Top

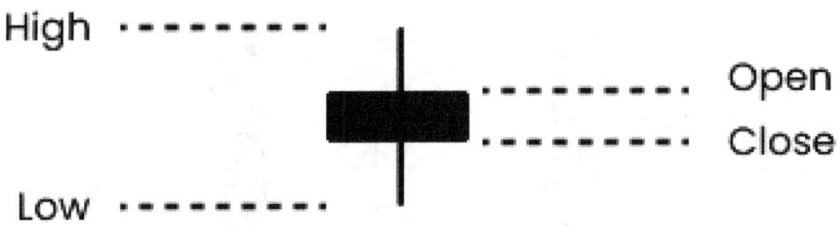

The spinning top pattern is a one-candle reversal pattern that indicates uncertainty in the market. It has a small body that closes in the middle of the candle's range, with long wicks on both sides. It can appear in both uptrends and downtrends and might indicate the conclusion of a period dominated by selling pressure.

Some see it as a reversal pattern, while others view it as a sign of market indecision. Confirming its significance requires additional filters and conditions, and analyzing the pattern should consider volume as a useful tool.

Falling Three Methods

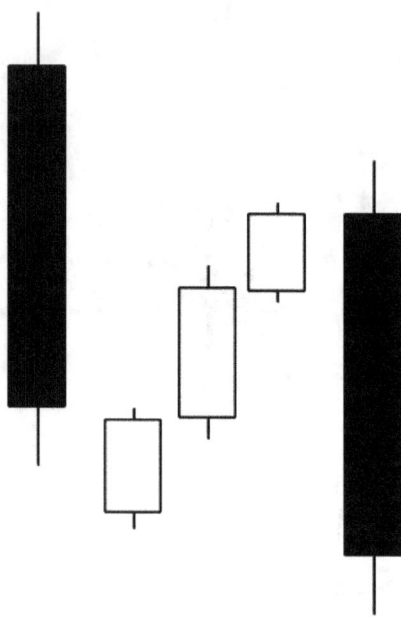

The Falling Three Methods is a bearish candlestick pattern that occurs during a downtrend. It consists of a long bearish candle, followed by three small bullish candles, and another long bearish candle. The small bullish candles are typically contained within the range of the first bearish candle.

This pattern indicates a temporary pause in the downtrend before the bears regain control. It suggests that the downward momentum is likely to continue after the pattern completes, potentially leading to further price declines.

Rising Three Methods

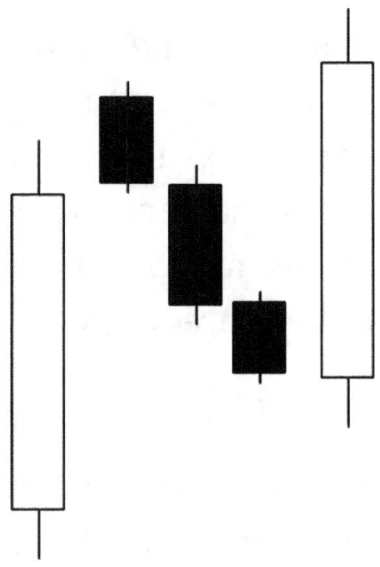

The Rising Three Methods is a bullish candlestick pattern characterized by a long white (green) candlestick followed by three small-bodied candlesticks contained within the range of the first candle. The first candle represents an uptrend, while the subsequent three candles indicate consolidation or a temporary pause in the trend.

This pattern suggests that the bullish trend is likely to continue after the consolidation period. Traders may interpret this pattern as a signal to enter or add to long positions, as it indicates a potential continuation of the upward movement.

Chart Patterns

Technical Analysis can't be done without chart patterns. It is a picture of how the price of an asset has changed over time. It is made by putting together the past and current prices of an asset. It shows how people as a group act on the price of securities and can help predict what prices might do next.

Traders who know how to read charts and use them to decide whether to buy or sell have a better chance of being on the right side of the trend. So, if you are starting in trading, you should learn how to recognize and understand Chart Patterns.

Chart patterns are "fractal in nature," which means that they can be used in any time frame, such as 15 minutes, 30 minutes, 1 hour, daily, weekly, monthly, and so on.

The first step to becoming a good trader is to train your eyes to spot chart patterns by looking at the price chart of any security. This needs to be done often. Make it a habit to look at charts of different assets every day.

Head and Shoulder

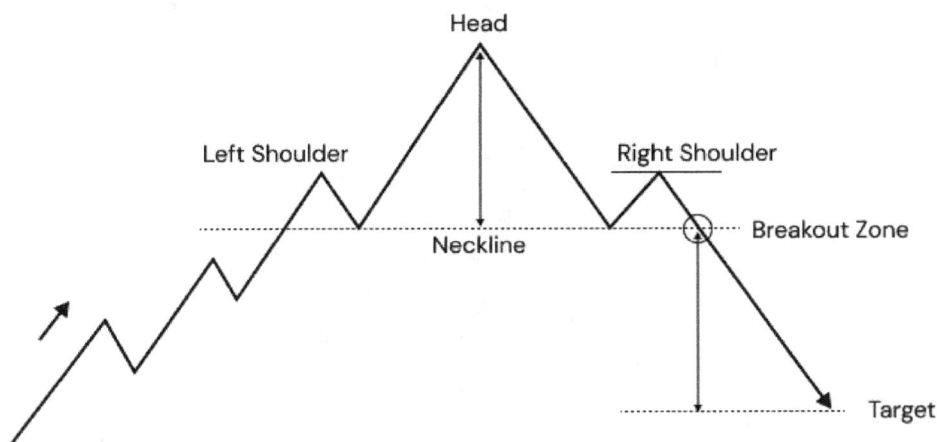

The Head and Shoulders pattern is a powerful reversal pattern that indicates the end of an uptrend. It consists of three peaks, with the middle peak (the head) being higher than the other two (the shoulders). The neckline connects the lows of the two shoulders.

When the price breaks below the neckline, it suggests a potential downtrend. Traders often use this pattern to predict future price movements and make trading decisions.

Chart Example of Head and Shoulders:

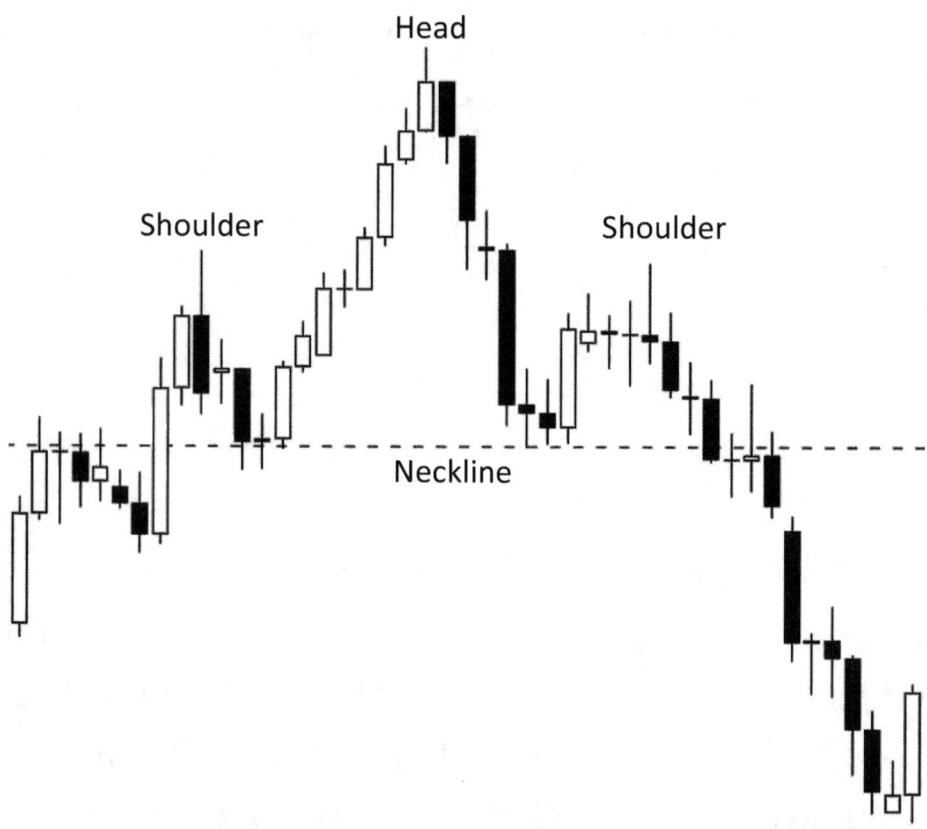

Inverted Head and Shoulder

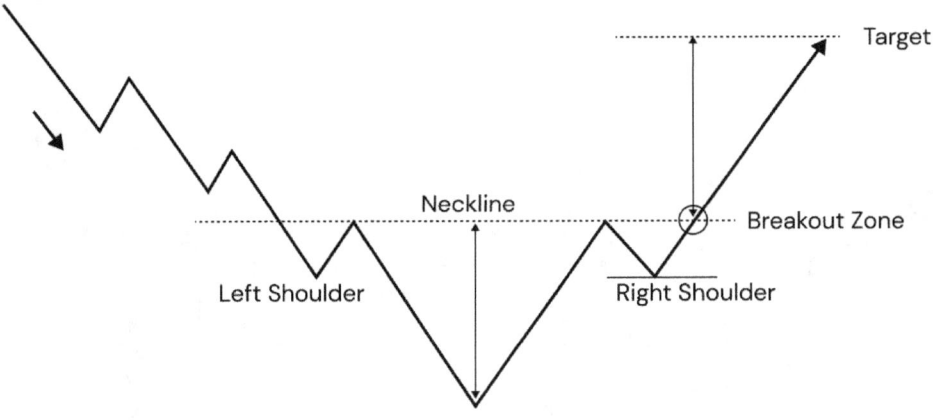

The Inverted Head and Shoulders pattern is a powerful reversal pattern that indicates the end of a downtrend. It is formed by three lows, with the middle low (the head) being lower than the two surrounding lows (the shoulders).

The pattern is completed when the price breaks above the neckline, which is a line drawn across the highs of the two shoulders. This pattern suggests a shift in market sentiment from bearish to bullish, and traders often interpret it as a signal to buy.

Chart Example of Inverted Head and Shoulders:

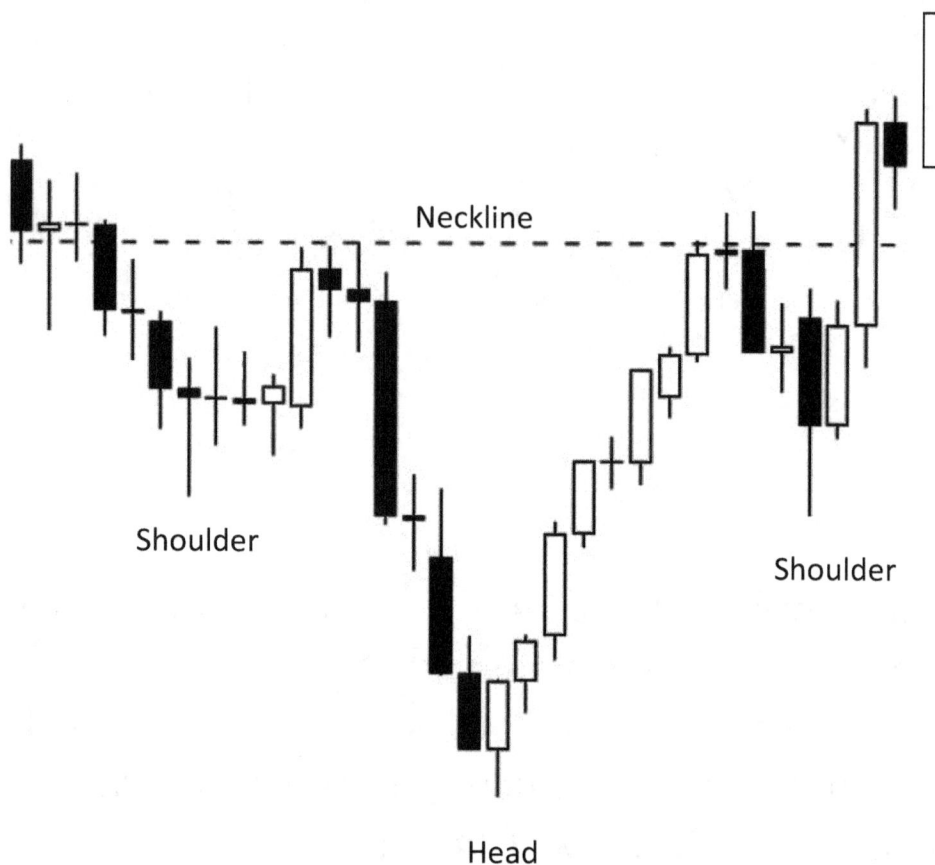

Neckline

Shoulder

Shoulder

Head

Double Top

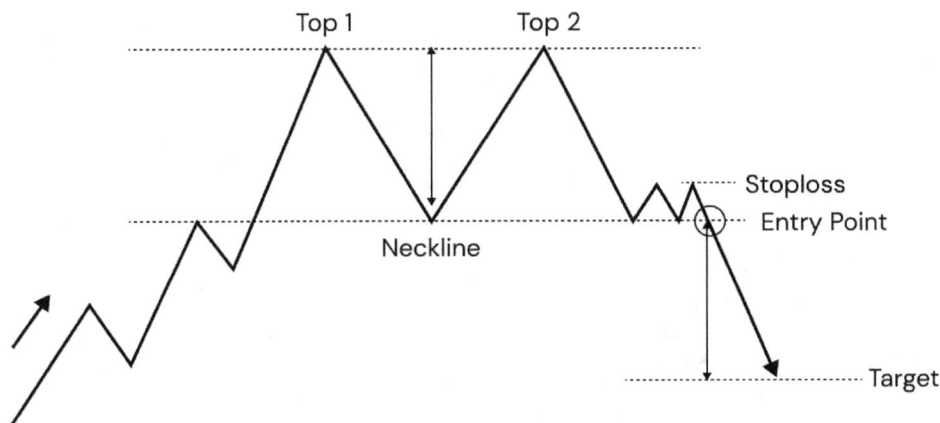

The double top pattern is a bearish reversal pattern that occurs in an uptrend. It consists of two consecutive peaks at approximately the same price level, with a neckline in between. The pattern suggests that the uptrend may be losing momentum and that a potential trend reversal is on the horizon.

Traders often look for a break below the neckline as confirmation of the pattern. The double top pattern can indicate a shift in sentiment from bullish to bearish, and traders may consider selling or shorting positions.

Chart Example of Double Top:

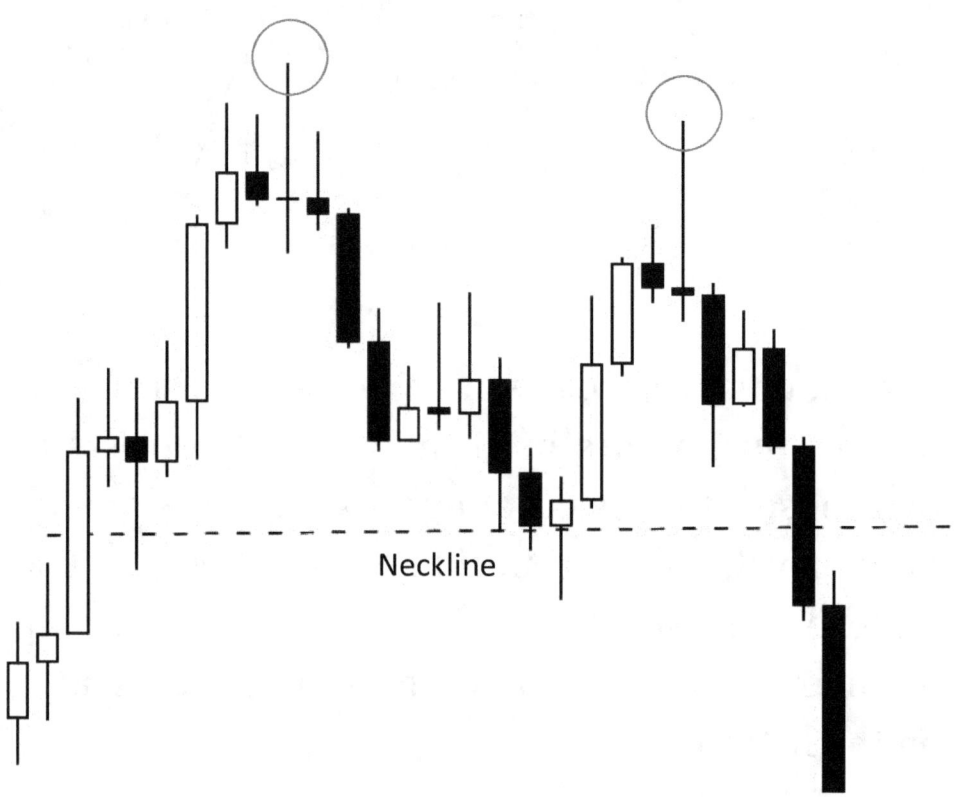

Neckline

Double Bottom

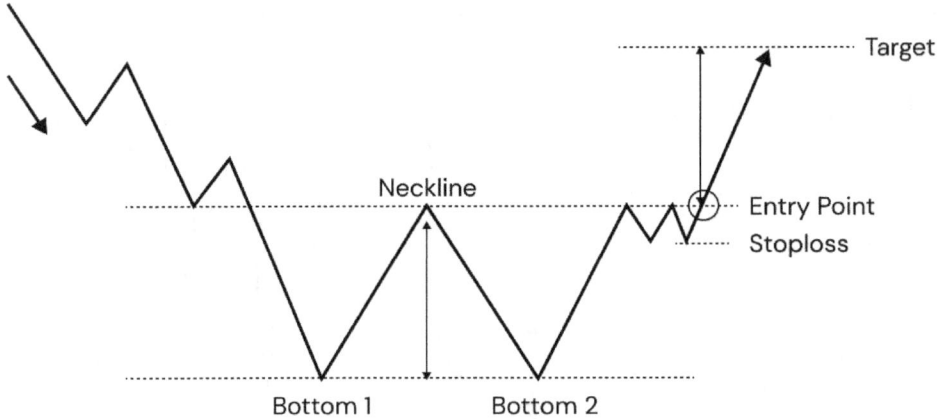

The Double Bottom pattern is a bullish reversal pattern that forms after a downtrend. It consists of two consecutive bottom of similar depth, with a peak in between. The pattern suggests that the downtrend may be ending and a new uptrend could begin.

Traders look for a break above the peak between the two bottoms to confirm the pattern. This breakout may signal a potential buying opportunity, with a target price set at the distance between the bottom and neckline added to the breakout point.

Chart Example of Double Bottom:

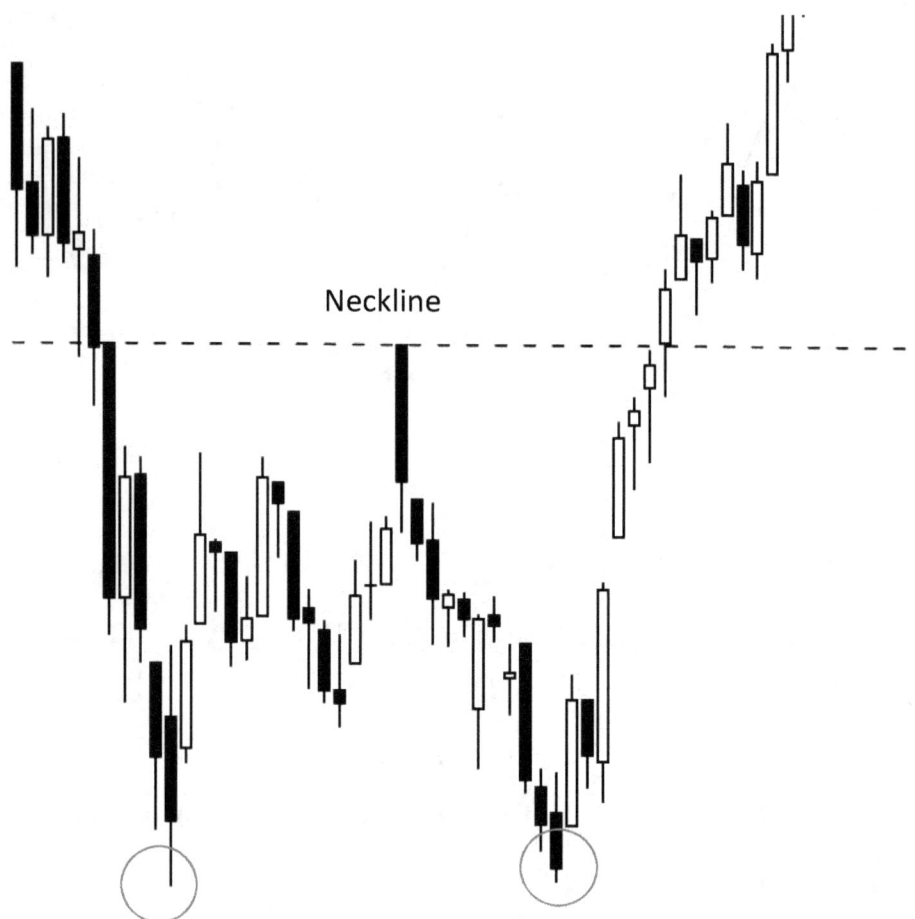

Neckline

Rounding Bottom

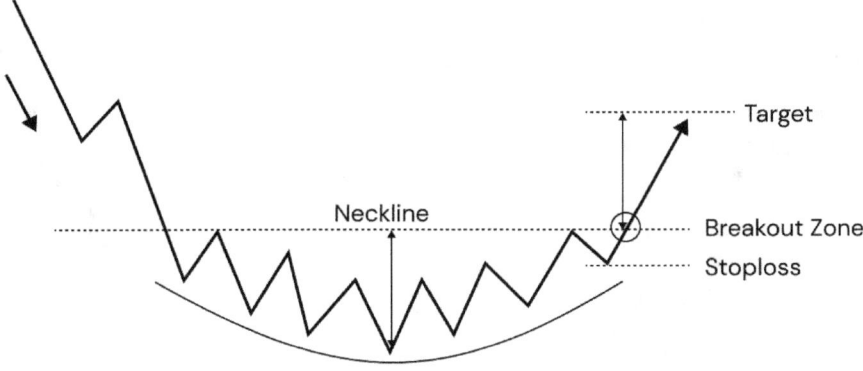

The rounding bottom pattern is a bullish reversal pattern that occurs when the price of an asset forms a rounded shape at the bottom of a downtrend. It is characterized by a gradual decline in price followed by a gradual increase, forming a "U" shape.

This pattern suggests that selling pressure is diminishing and buying pressure is increasing, indicating a potential trend reversal. Traders often look for confirmation signals, like a break above the pattern's neckline to enter long positions.

Chart Example of Rounding Bottom:

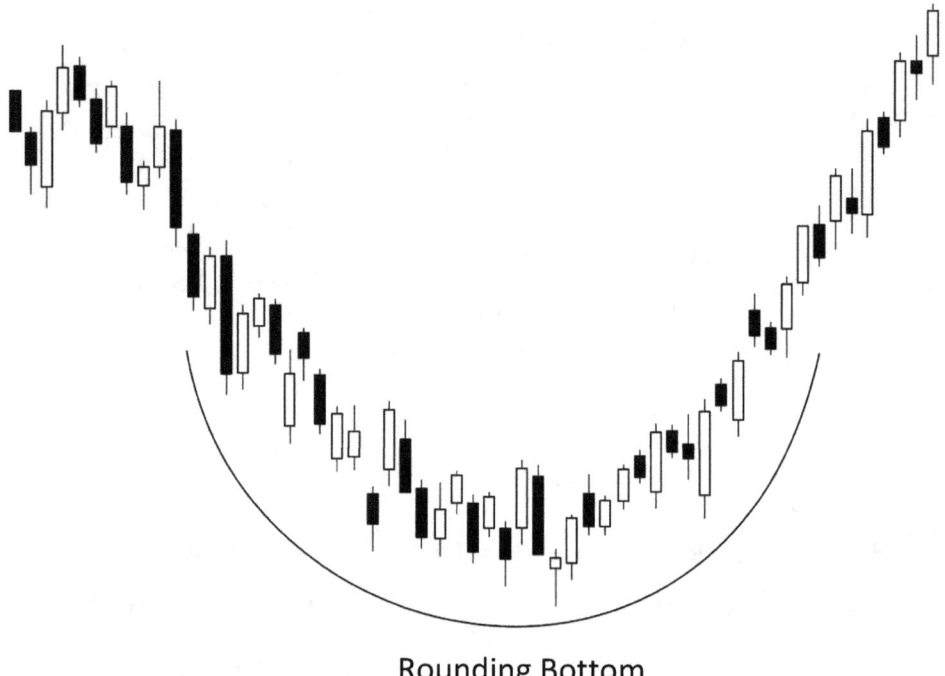

Rounding Bottom

Rounding Top

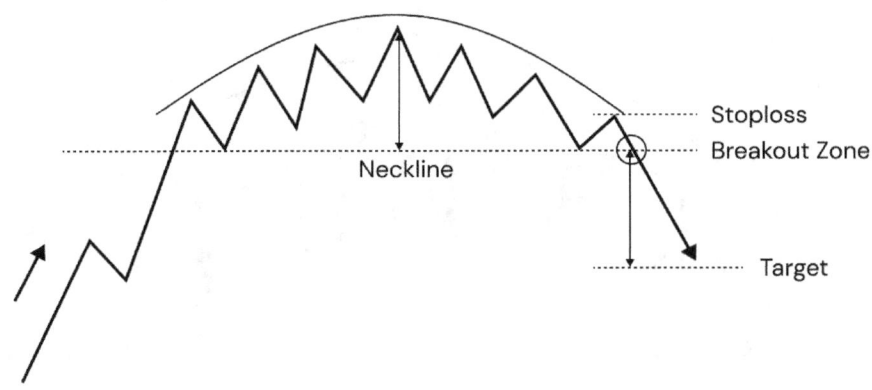

The rounding top pattern is a bearish reversal pattern that occurs at the end of a bullish trend. It is characterized by prices slowing down and rounding off at the top of an uptrend, resembling a dome or rounded hill. This indicates a decrease in bullish momentum and a weakening of the uptrend.

A downward breakout occurs when prices break through the support trendline, marking the end of the previous uptrend. Traders can identify this pattern by looking for a gradual curve in price movement, followed by a break below the neckline.

Chart Example of Rounding Top:

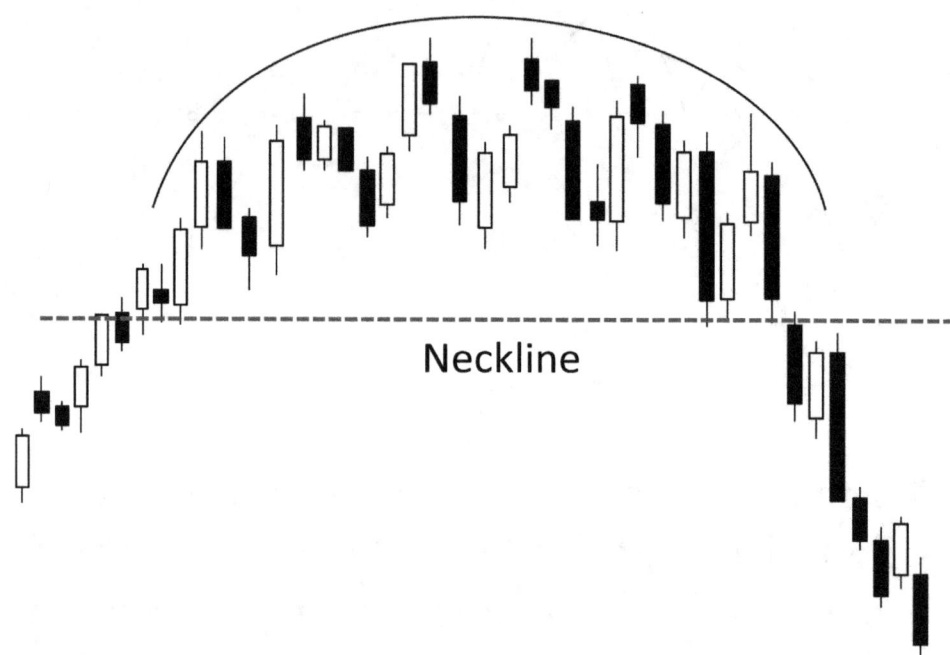

Neckline

Ascending Triangle

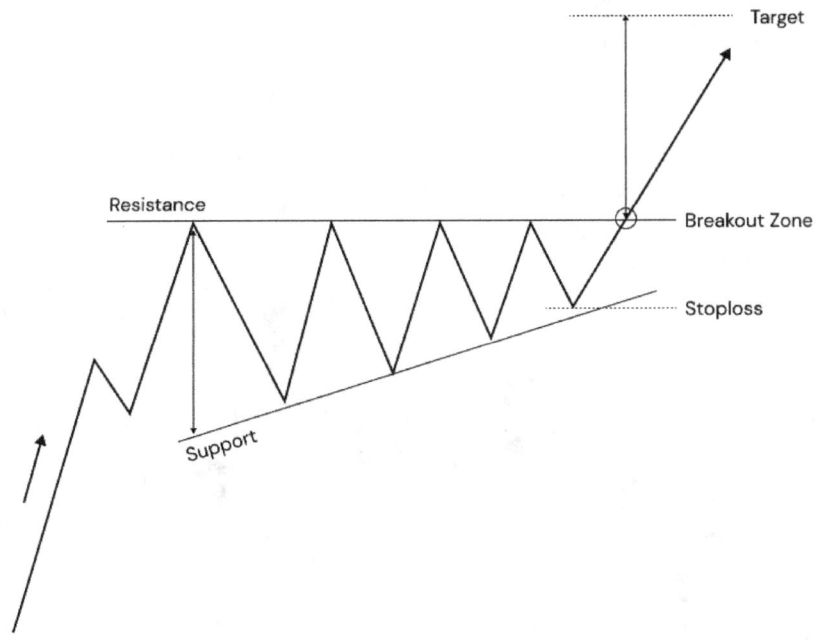

The ascending triangle pattern is a bullish continuation pattern that forms when there is a horizontal resistance level and a rising trendline. It is created by connecting a series of higher lows with a horizontal line representing the resistance level.

Traders look for a breakout above the resistance level as a signal to enter long positions, with the potential for the price to move higher. The pattern suggests that buying pressure is gradually overcoming selling pressure, indicating a potential upward trend continuation.

Chart Example of Ascending Triangle:

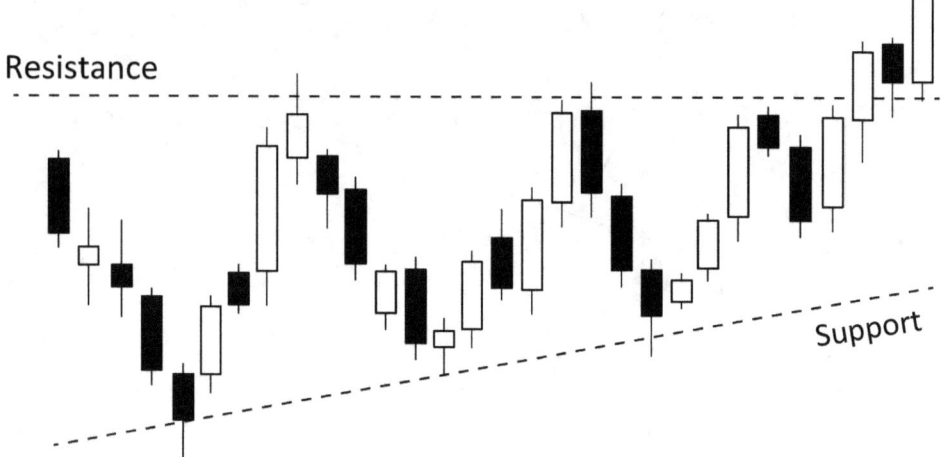

Resistance

Support

Descending Triangle

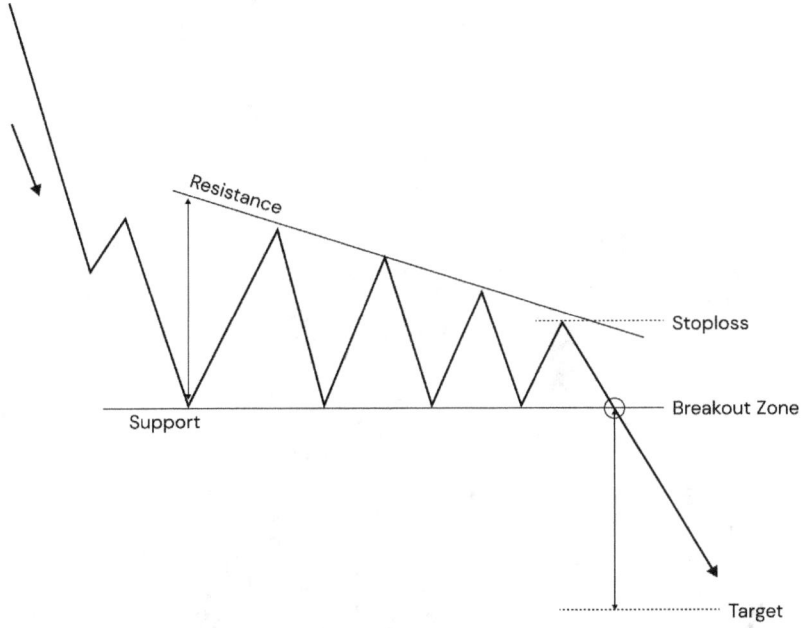

The descending triangle pattern is a bearish continuation pattern that forms during a downtrend. It is characterized by a horizontal support line and a descending trendline. The pattern suggests that sellers are in control and that the price is likely to continue falling.

Traders look for a breakdown below the support line as a confirmation signal to enter short positions. Traders usually set the profit target by measuring the height of the triangle and projecting it downward.

Chart Example of Descending Triangle:

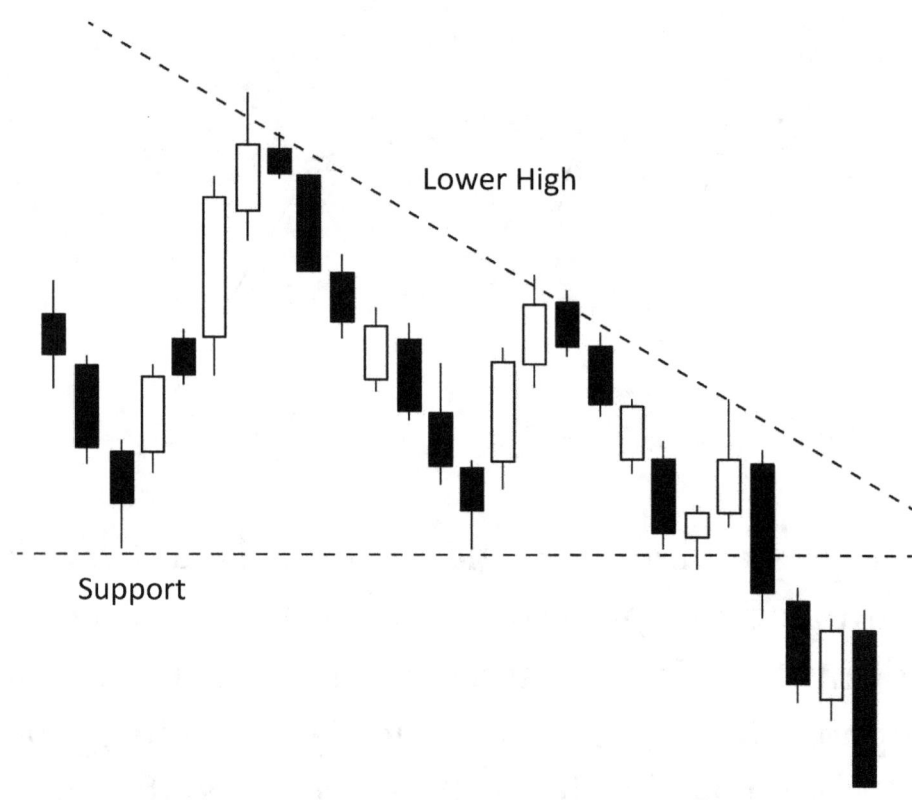

Bullish Rectangle

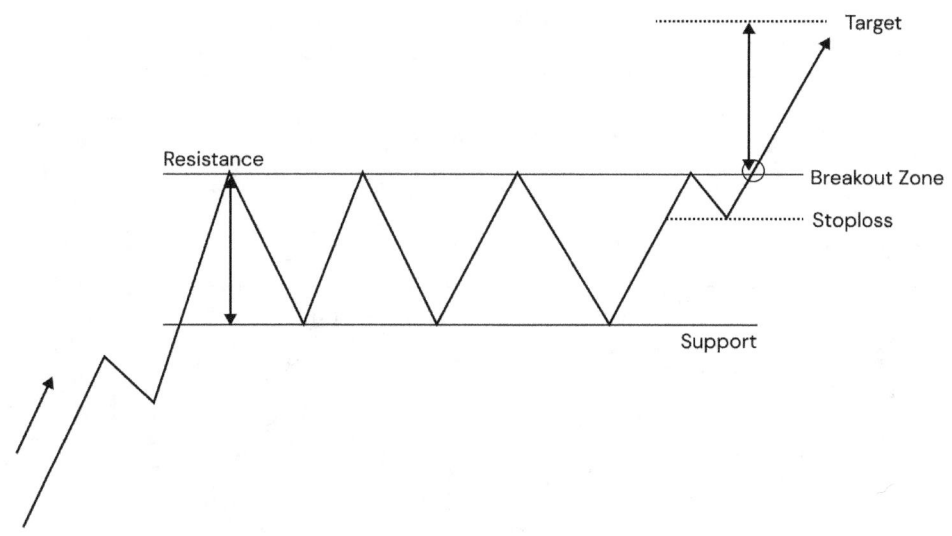

The bullish rectangle pattern is a chart pattern characterized by parallel support and resistance levels. It forms during an uptrend and indicates a period of consolidation or indecision. Traders look for a breakout above the resistance level, which confirms the bullish bias.

This pattern suggests a continuation of the uptrend, and traders often target a price move that is at least the size of the rectangle. It is important for traders to understand the key features of the bullish rectangle pattern to identify potential bullish breakouts and take advantage of the trend.

Chart Example of Bullish Rectangle:

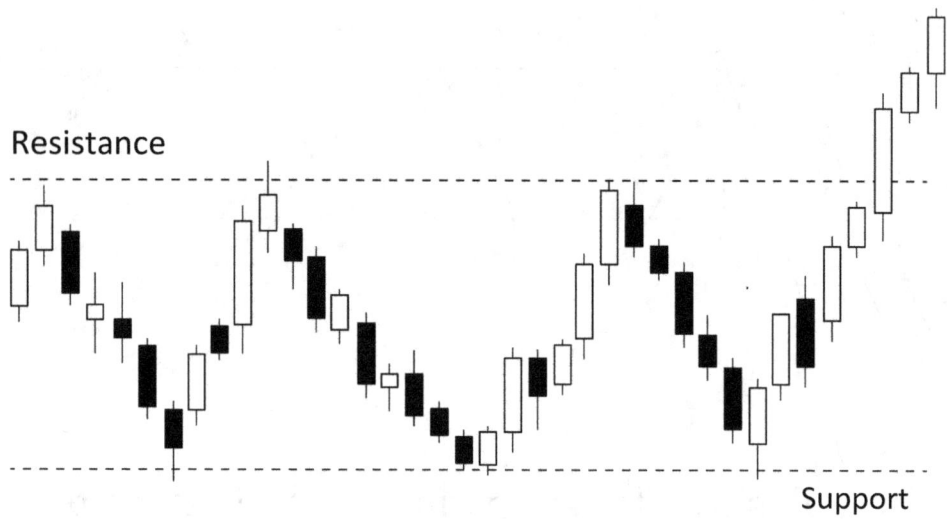

Resistance

Support

Bearish Rectangle

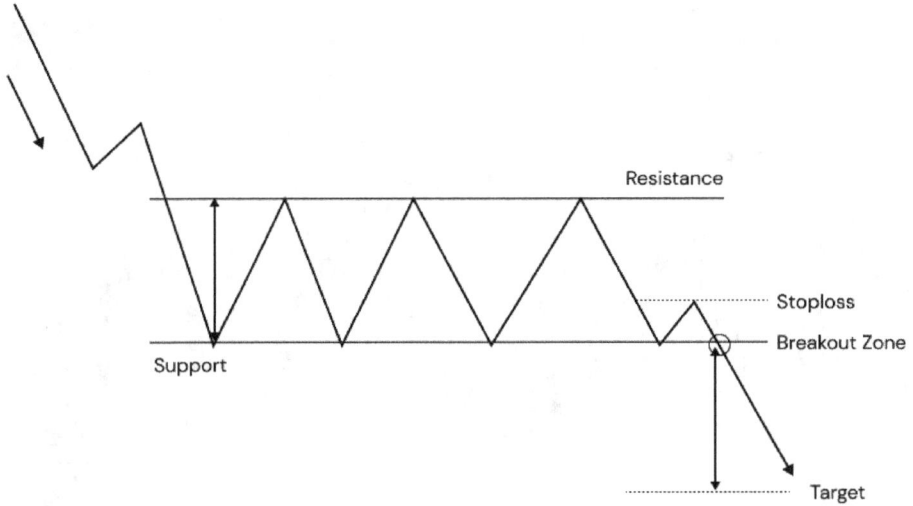

A bearish rectangle pattern is a chart pattern that indicates a potential continuation of a downtrend. It forms when the price oscillates between two horizontal lines, creating a rectangular shape. The upper line acts as resistance, while the lower line acts as support.

This pattern suggests indecision in the market, with buyers and sellers in balance. Traders often wait for a breakout below the support line to confirm the pattern. A bearish rectangle pattern can be an opportunity to enter a short position, targeting a price decline similar to the height of the rectangle.

Chart Example of Bearish Rectangle:

Resistance

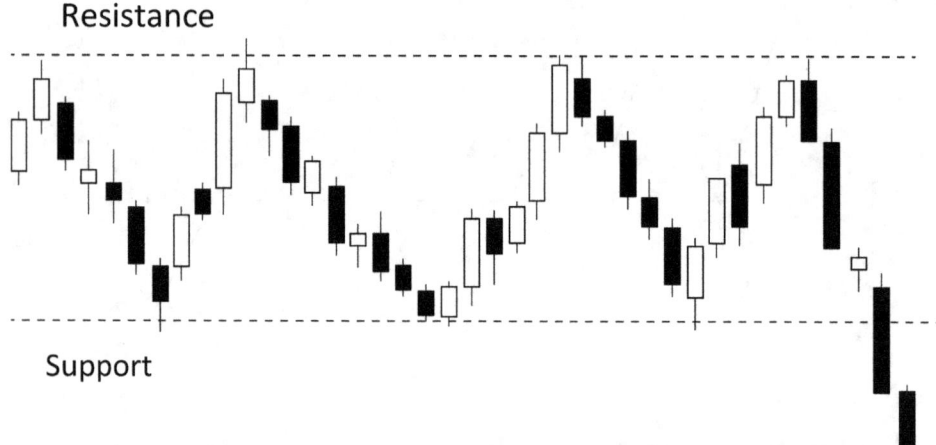

Support

Cup and Handle

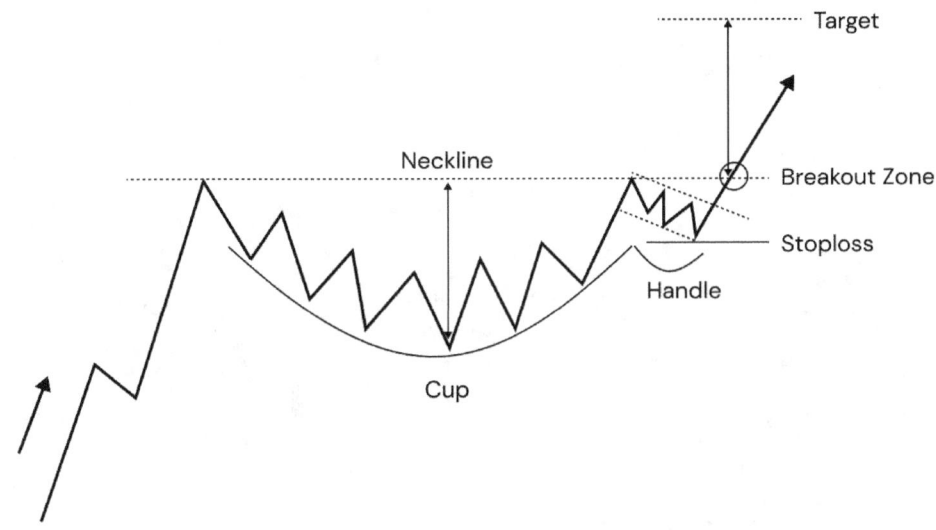

The cup and handle pattern is a bullish signal in trading. It consists of a U-shaped cup followed by a downward sloping handle. The pattern indicates a potential increase in price and provides trading opportunities. To trade on this pattern, traders should correctly identify it, set entry and exit points, and manage risk with stop losses.

The pattern is characterized by a rounded cup with at least one-third the depth of the previous uptrend and a downward-sloping handle. Traders should wait for the handle's pullback to finish and enter when the handle breaks.

Chart Example of Cup and Handle:

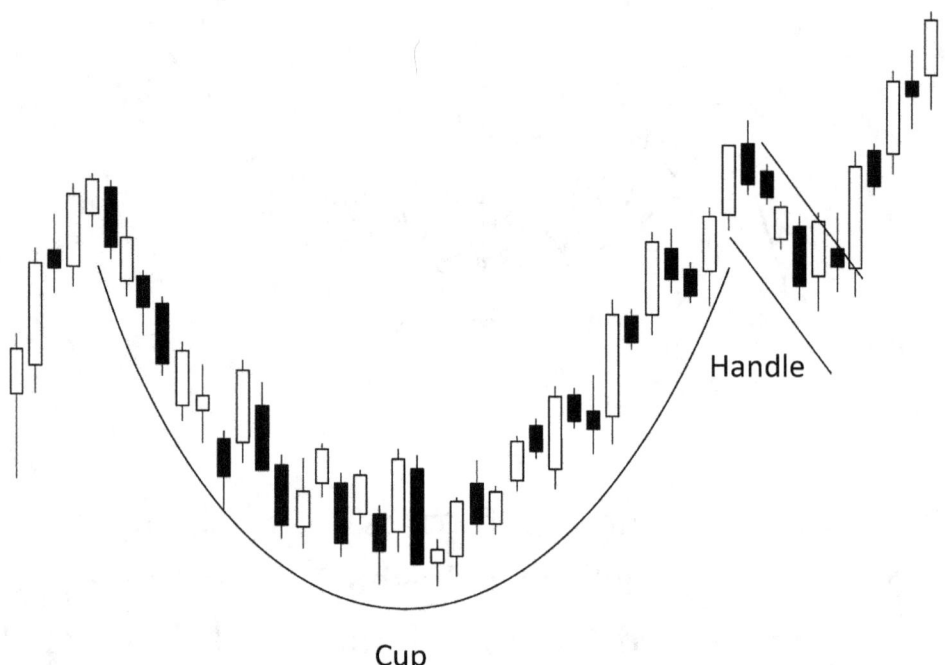

Handle

Cup

Inverted Cup and Handle

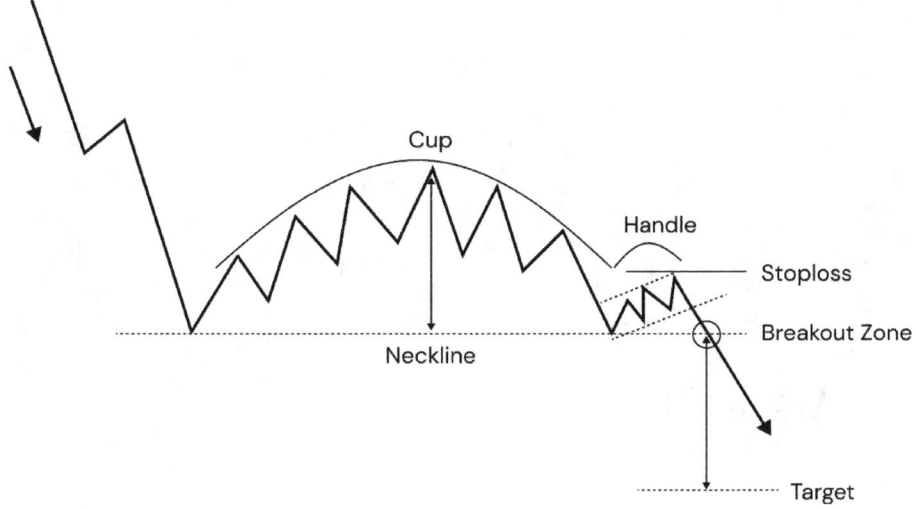

The inverted cup and handle pattern is a bearish reversal pattern that appears in an upward price trend. It consists of a rounded top, followed by a sharp price decline and consolidation, forming the handle. This pattern can be confirmed when the base of the cup breaks.

Traders can take short positions once the base of the cup breaks and holds, placing a stop at the top of the handle.

Chart Example of Inverted Cup and Handle:

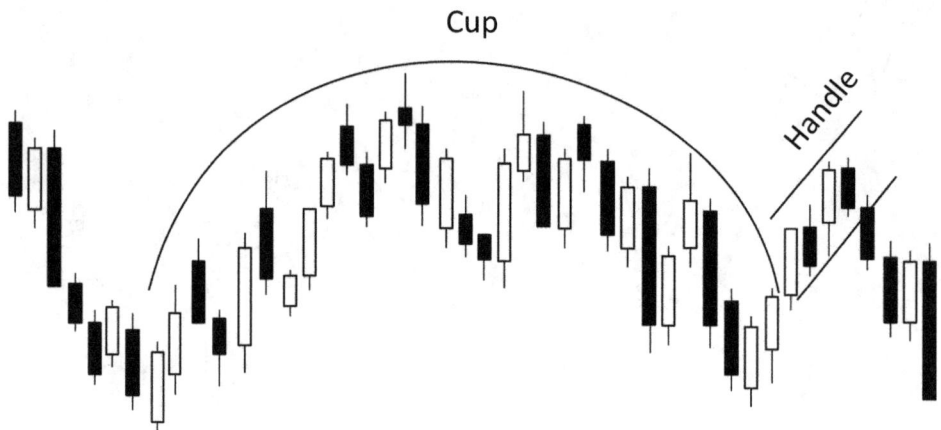

Cup

Handle

Rising Channel

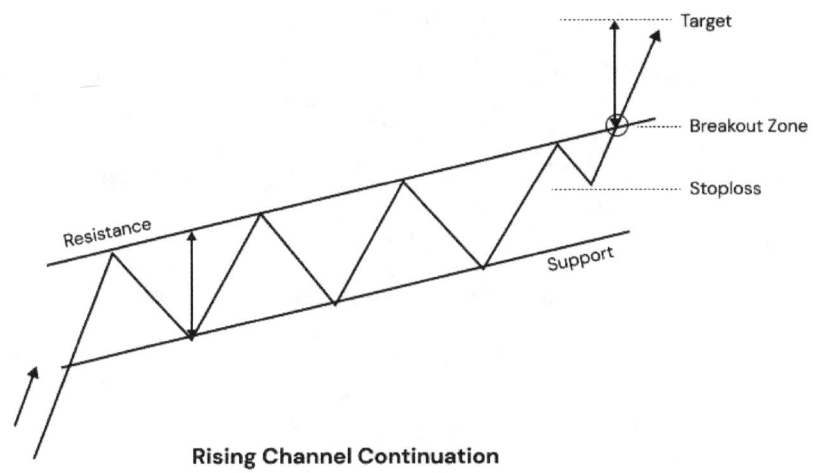

Rising Channel Continuation

The rising channel chart pattern is characterized by two upward sloping parallel trend lines. It indicates an increase in the price of an asset. Traders can use the channel's support and resistance levels to set stop-loss orders and profit targets. They can also trade in the direction of channel breakouts or breakdowns.

A long position can be opened when the price reaches the lower trend line and exited when it approaches the upper trend line. Breakouts above the upper trend line and breakdowns below the lower trend line, respectively, can indicate a trend continuation or a possible trend change.

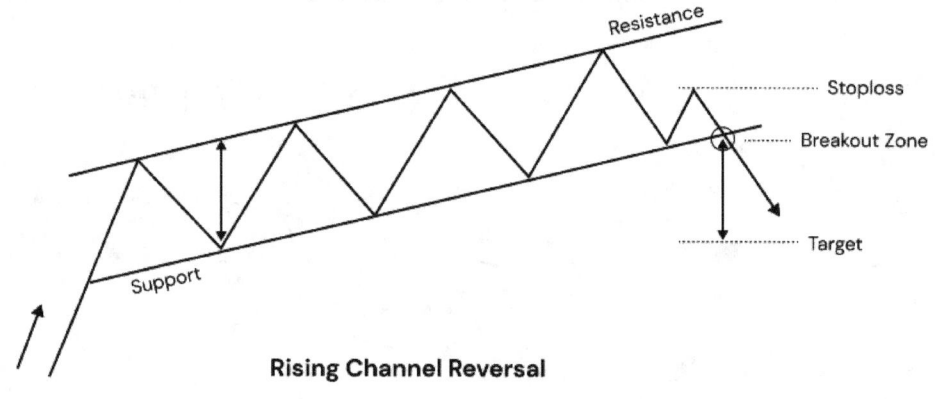

Rising Channel Reversal

Chart Example of Rising Channel:

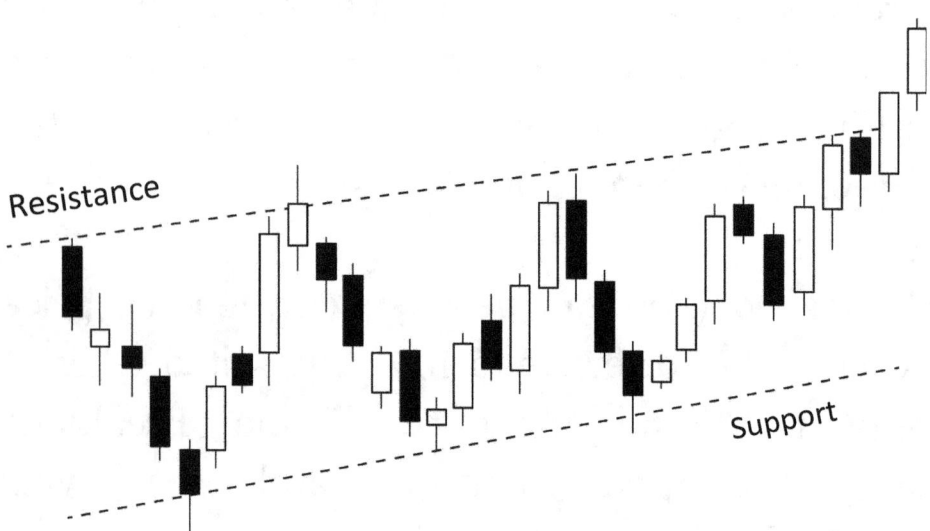

Falling Channel

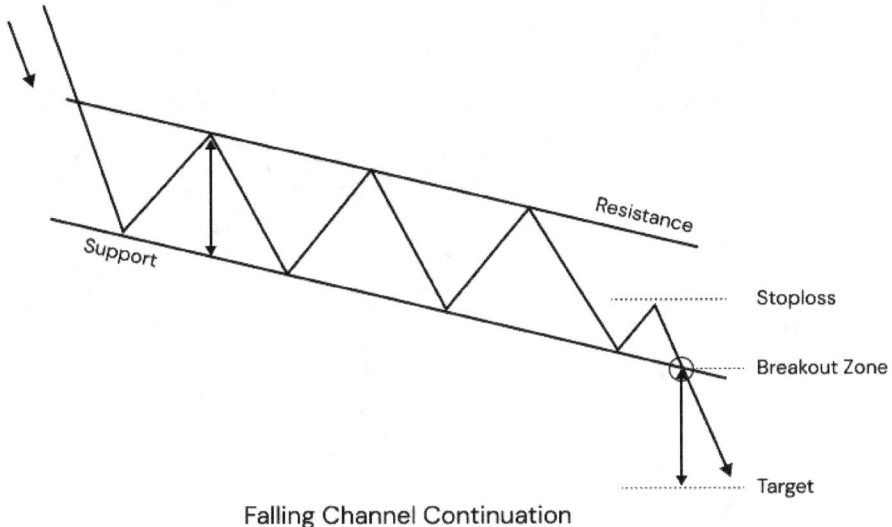

Falling Channel Continuation

The falling channel pattern is a bearish chart pattern that is characterized by two downward-sloping trend lines. The upper trend line connects the swing highs, while the lower trend line connects the swing lows. The price tends to move within these two trend lines, indicating a downtrend.

Traders often look for opportunities to sell when the price reaches the upper trend line and place stop-loss orders above the upper trend line. This pattern suggests that the downtrend is likely to continue.

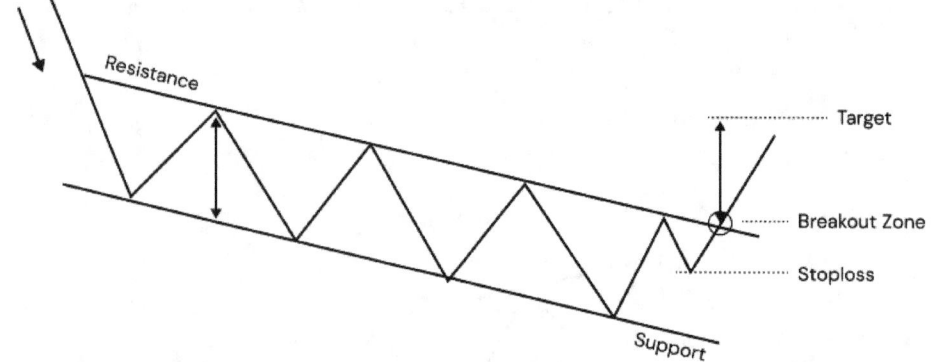

Falling Channel Reversal

Chart Example of Falling Channel:

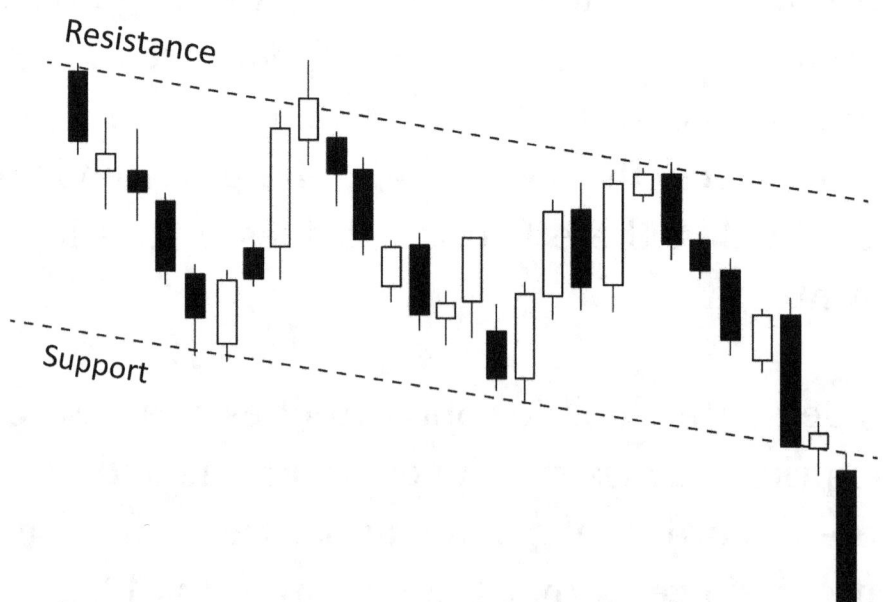

Rising Wedge

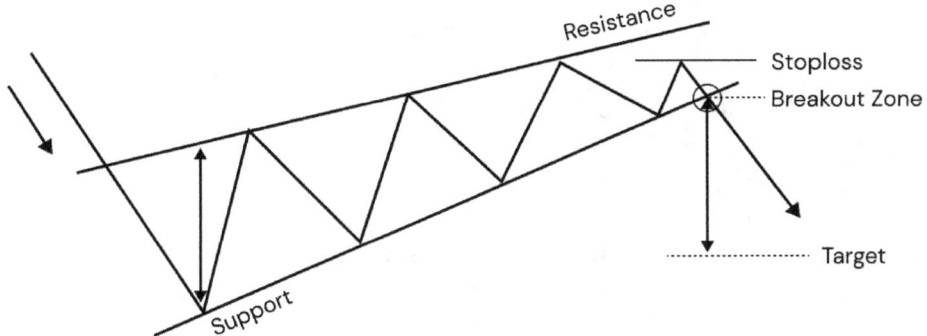

Rising Wedge Continuation

The rising wedge pattern is a chart pattern that signals a potential reversal in an uptrend. It is formed by drawing two converging trendlines, with the upper trendline showing higher highs and the lower trendline showing higher lows. This pattern indicates that buying pressure is weakening, and sellers may take control soon.

Traders often interpret a breakout below the lower trendline as a bearish signal, suggesting a potential downward move. However, it is essential to consider other indicators and confirm the pattern before making trading decisions.

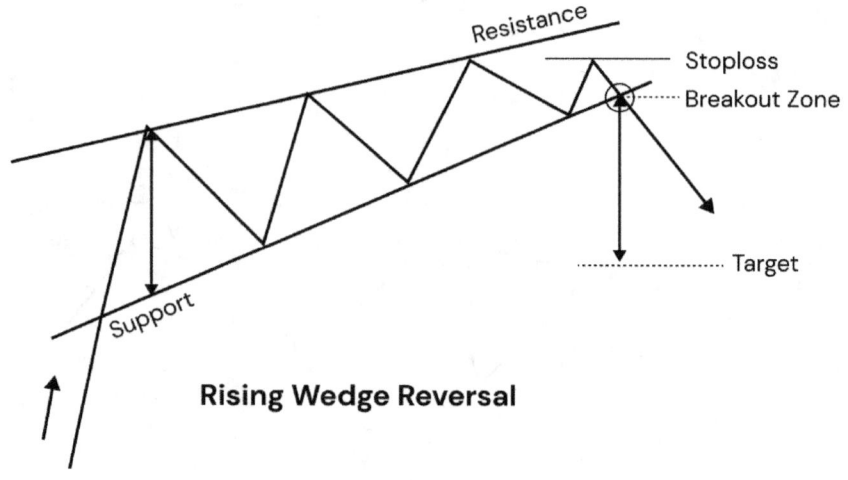

Rising Wedge Reversal

Chart Example of Rising Wedge:

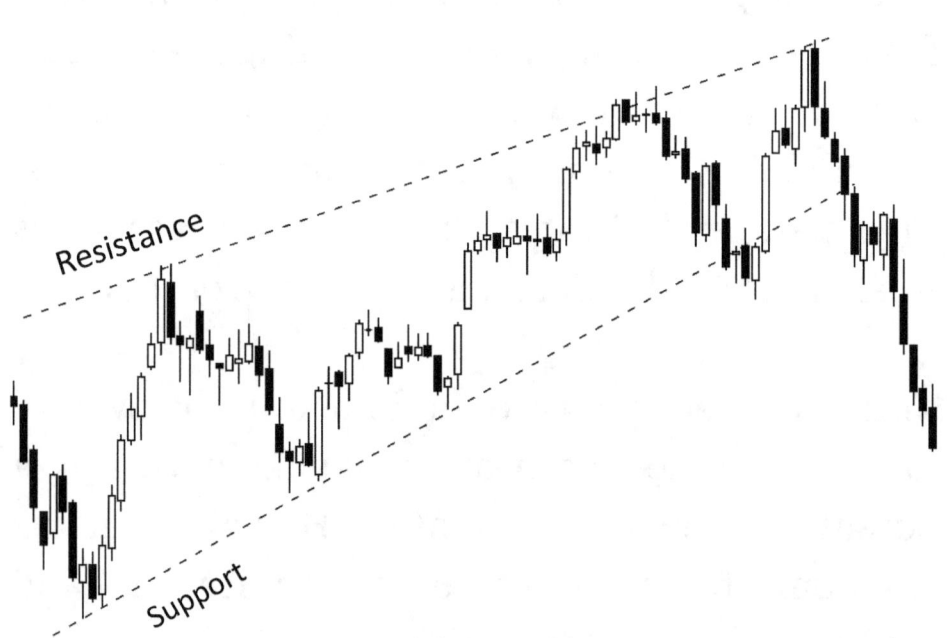

Falling Wedge

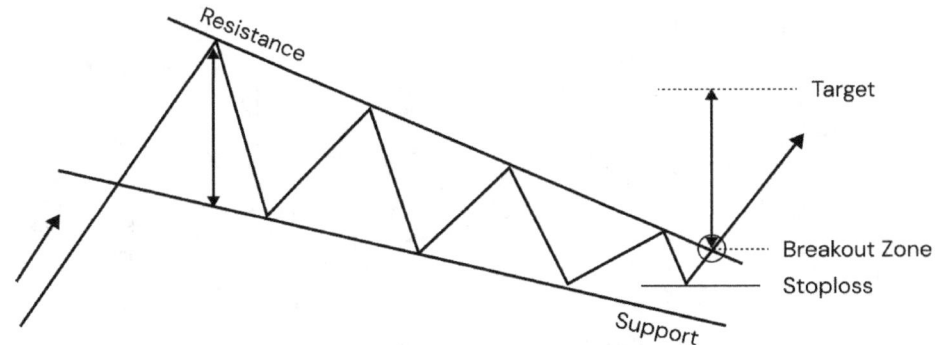

Falling Wedge Continuation

The falling wedge pattern is a chart pattern that signals a potential reversal in a downtrend. It is formed by drawing two converging trendlines, with the upper trendline showing lower highs and the lower trendline showing lower lows.

This pattern indicates weakening selling pressure and suggests that buyers may take control soon. Traders often interpret a breakout above the upper trendline as a bullish signal, indicating a potential upward move.

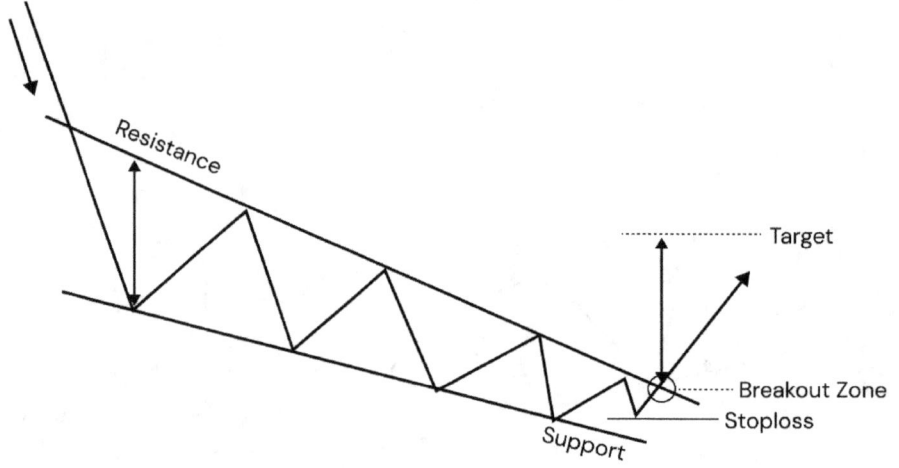

Falling Wedge Reversal

Chart Example of Falling Wedge:

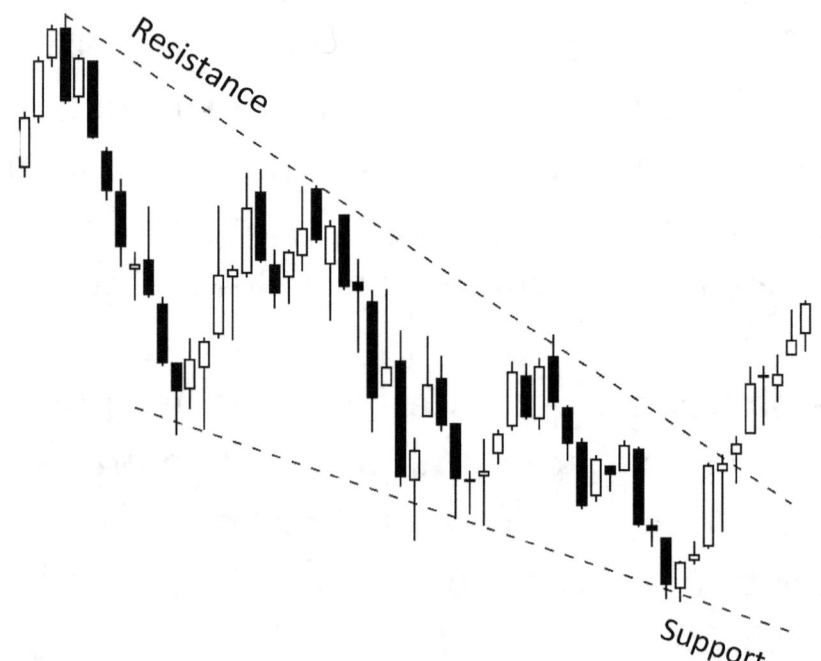

Symmetrical Triangle

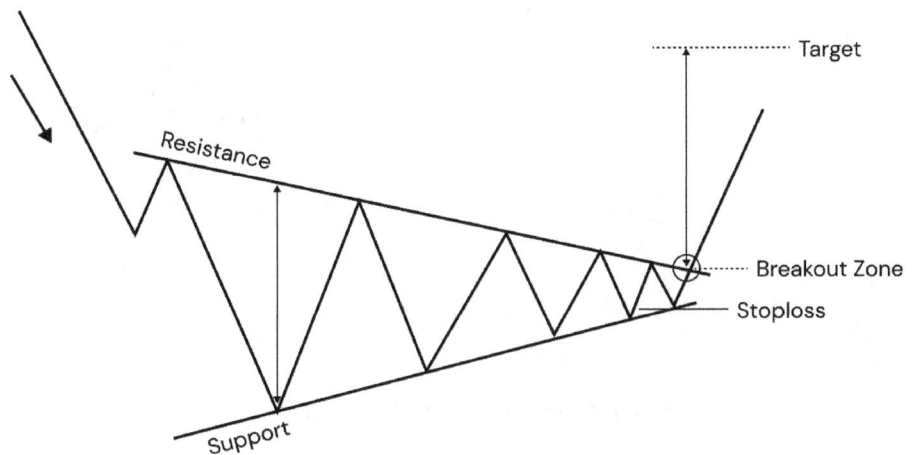

Bullish Reversal Symmetrical Triangle

The symmetrical triangle pattern is a neutral chart formation that indicates a period of price consolidation before a potential breakout. It is formed by two converging trendlines, with at least two lower highs and two higher lows. The pattern suggests that the market is undecided about its future direction.

Breakouts from the pattern are often accompanied by strong volume and are more likely to occur in the direction of the prevailing trend. Traders should pay attention to the overall message of the market rather than the exact shape of the pattern.

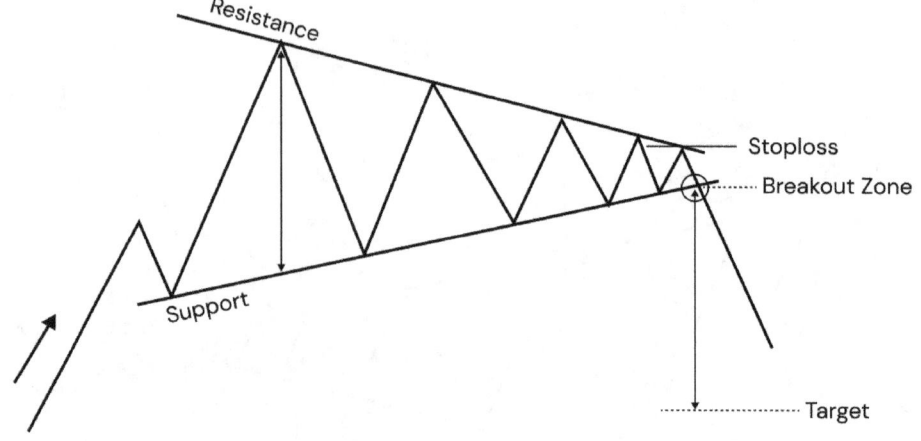

Bullish Reversal Symmetrical Triangle

Chart Example of Symmetrical Triangle:

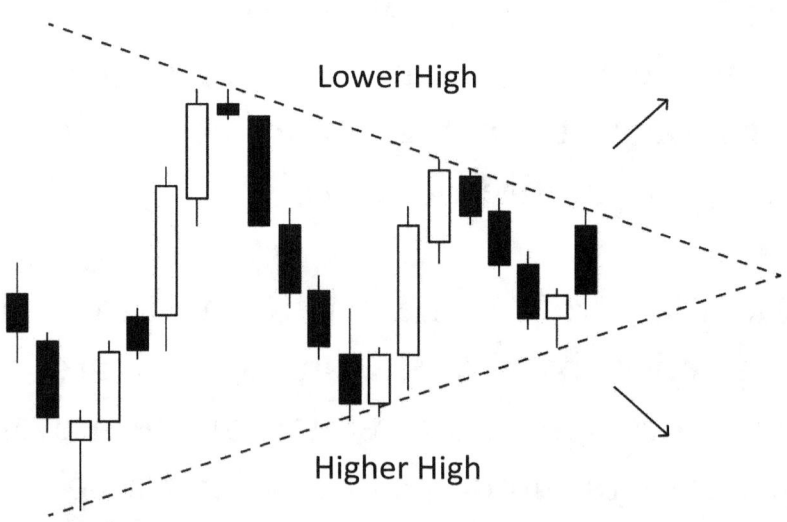

Pennant or Flag

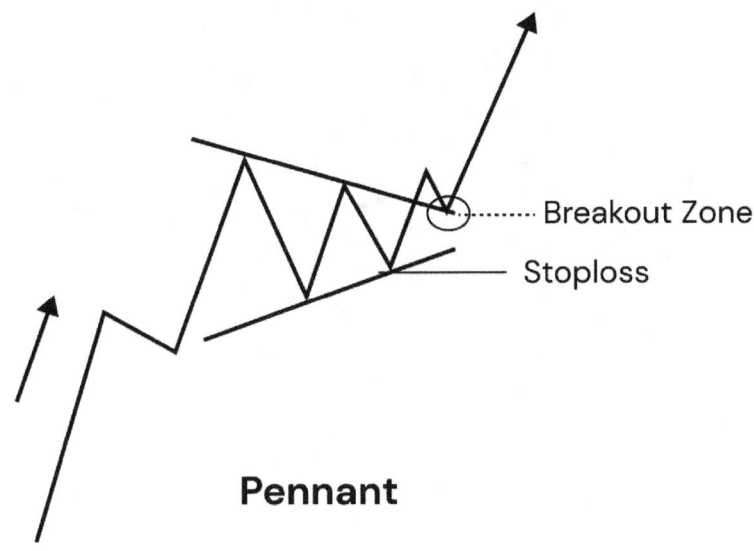

Breakout Zone

Stoploss

Pennant

The pennant and flag patterns are both continuation patterns that occur after a strong price movement. In the pennant pattern, the price consolidates in a small symmetrical triangle shape before continuing in the direction of the previous trend. The flag pattern is similar but has a rectangular shape.

Both patterns indicate a temporary pause in the market before the trend resumes. Traders should look for confirmation signals and consider other indicators before making trading decisions based on these patterns.

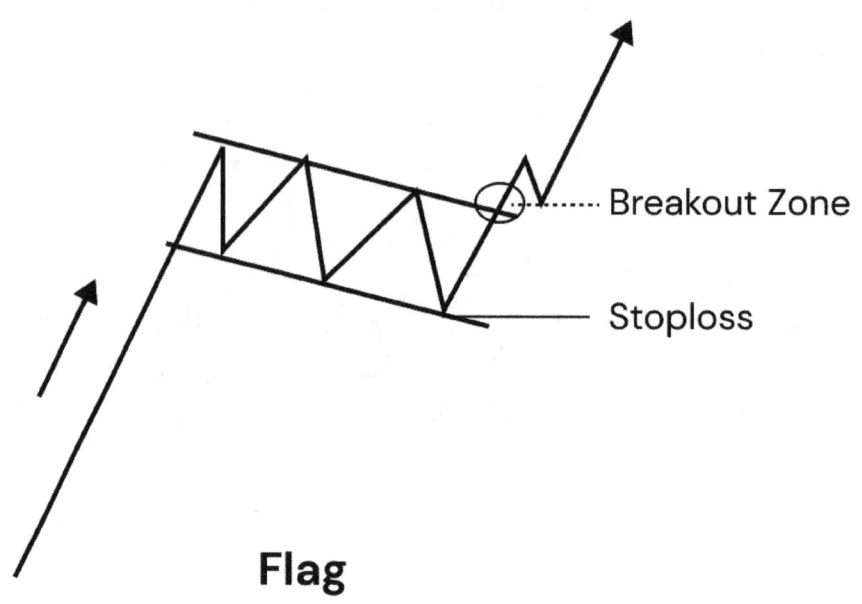

Flag

Chart Example of Pennant:

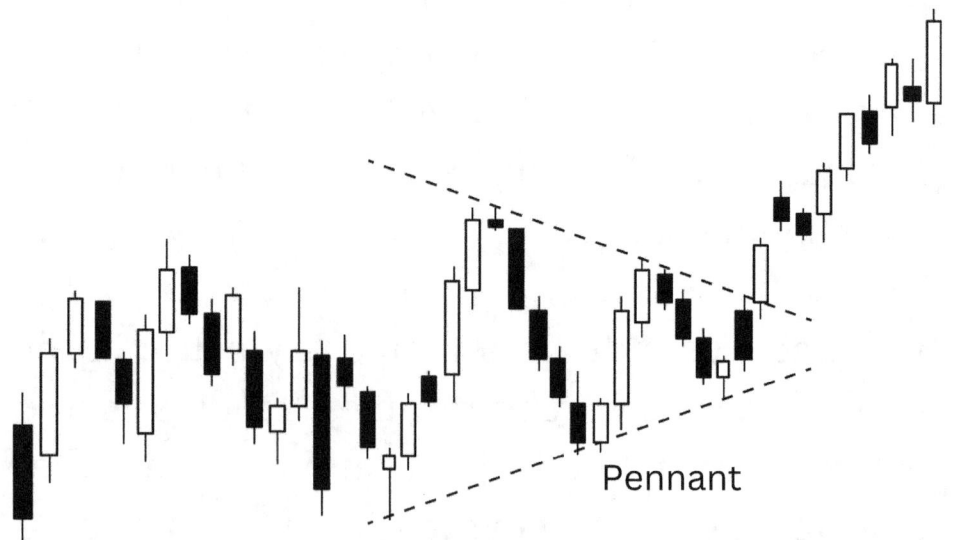

Pennant

Indicators

Indicators are tools or mathematical calculations that traders use to analyze and interpret market data in order to make informed decisions about buying or selling financial instruments such as stocks, currencies, commodities, or cryptocurrencies. These indicators are derived from historical price and volume data and are intended to provide insight into market trends, volatility, momentum, and other price movement aspects.

I discussed Some Common Indicators.

- Moving Averages
- MACD
- RSI
- Fibonacci Retracements

Moving Averages

Moving Averages (MA) is a popular technical analysis tool used to analyze trend direction and potential support and resistance levels in financial markets. It is calculated by averaging the closing prices of a security over a specified period of time, creating a smoothed line that represents the average price over that period. The most commonly used moving averages are the Simple Moving Average (SMA) and the Exponential Moving Average (EMA).

Traders use moving averages to identify trends, generate buy or sell signals, and set stop-loss levels. Short-term moving averages respond quickly to price changes, while long-term moving averages provide a more smoothed-out view of the trend.

How to trade with the RSI indicator:

1. Determine the trend: Use moving averages to identify the direction of the trend. When the shorter-term moving average crosses above the longer-term moving average, it indicates an uptrend, and vice versa for a downtrend.

2. Entry signals: Wait for a pullback or a retracement within the trend. When the price touches or crosses above the moving average during an uptrend, it may signal a buy entry. Conversely, during a downtrend, a touch or cross below the moving average could indicate a sell entry.

MACD

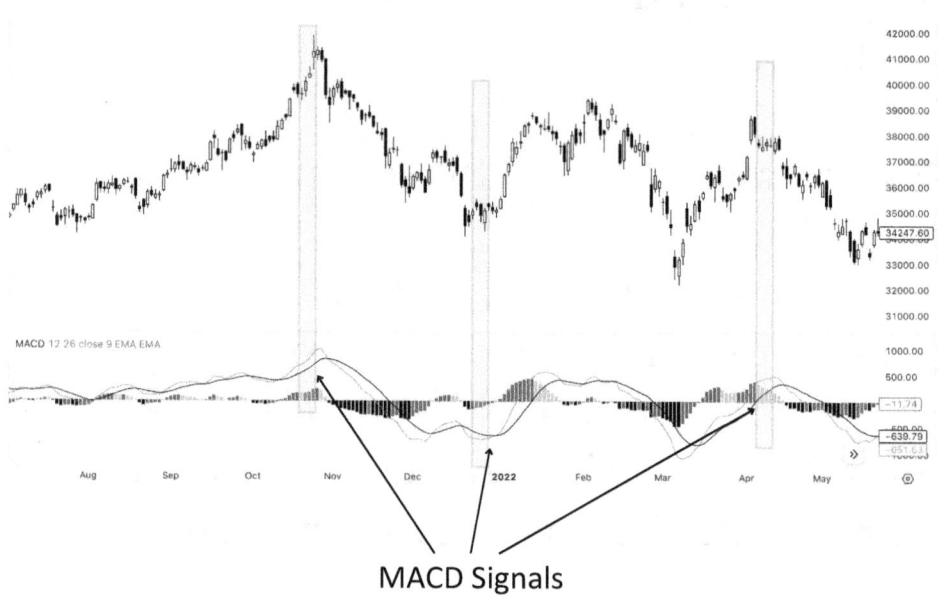

MACD Signals

The Moving Average Convergence Divergence (MACD) is a popular technical indicator used by traders to identify trends and momentum in the market. It calculates the difference between two moving averages of a security's price and can be used in various markets. The MACD consists of three components: the MACD line, the signal line, and the histogram.

Traders can use the MACD indicator to identify entry and exit points for trades. However, it is less useful for stocks that are not trending or have unpredictable price action. The MACD was invented by Gerald Appel.

Here's a simple way to trade with the MACD indicator:

1. Look for a bullish signal: When the MACD line (the faster line) crosses above the signal line (the slower line), it generates a bullish signal. This indicates a potential buying opportunity.

2. Look for a bearish signal: When the MACD line crosses below the signal line, it generates a bearish signal. This indicates a potential selling opportunity.

3. Confirm with price action: It's important to confirm the MACD signal by analyzing price action and other indicators. Look for additional signs of trend reversal or continuation.

Set stop-loss and take-profit levels: Determine your risk tolerance and set appropriate stop-loss and take-profit levels to manage your trade effectively.

Remember, the MACD indicator should not be used in isolation. It is best used in conjunction with other technical indicators and analysis methods to increase the probability of successful trades.

RSI

The Relative Strength Index (RSI) is a momentum indicator used in technical analysis to evaluate overvalued or undervalued conditions in the price of a security. It measures the speed and magnitude of recent price changes and is displayed as an oscillator on a scale of zero to 100. An RSI reading of 70 or above indicates an overbought situation, while a reading of 30 or below indicates an oversold condition.

The RSI can also signal trend reversals or corrective pullbacks in price, providing buy and sell signals. It works best in trading ranges rather than trending markets and can be used in conjunction with other technical indicators to support trading strategies.

How to trade with the RSI indicator:

1. Identify overbought and oversold levels: RSI ranges from 0 to 100, with values above 70 indicating overbought conditions and values below 30 indicating oversold conditions.

2. Look for divergence: If the price is making higher highs while the RSI is making lower highs, it could be a bearish divergence. Conversely, if the price is making lower lows while the RSI is making higher lows, it could be a bullish divergence.

3. Use RSI crossovers: When the RSI crosses above 30, it could be a bullish signal. When it crosses below 70, it could be a bearish signal.

Fibonacci Retracements

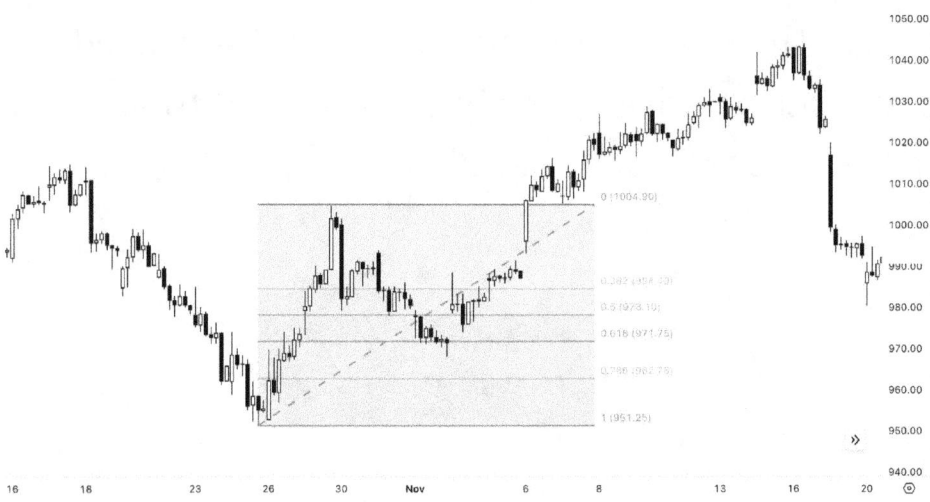

Fibonacci retracement levels are horizontal lines used in technical analysis to indicate potential support and resistance levels in financial markets. These levels are derived from the Fibonacci sequence and are associated with percentages such as 23.6%, 38.2%, 50%, 61.8%, and 78.6%.

Traders use Fibonacci retracements to draw support and resistance lines, place stop-loss orders, set price targets, and identify potential reversal points. However, the use of Fibonacci retracements is subjective and some traders argue that it is unreliable. It is best used in conjunction with other indicators and tools for a more comprehensive analysis.

Breakout and Pullback

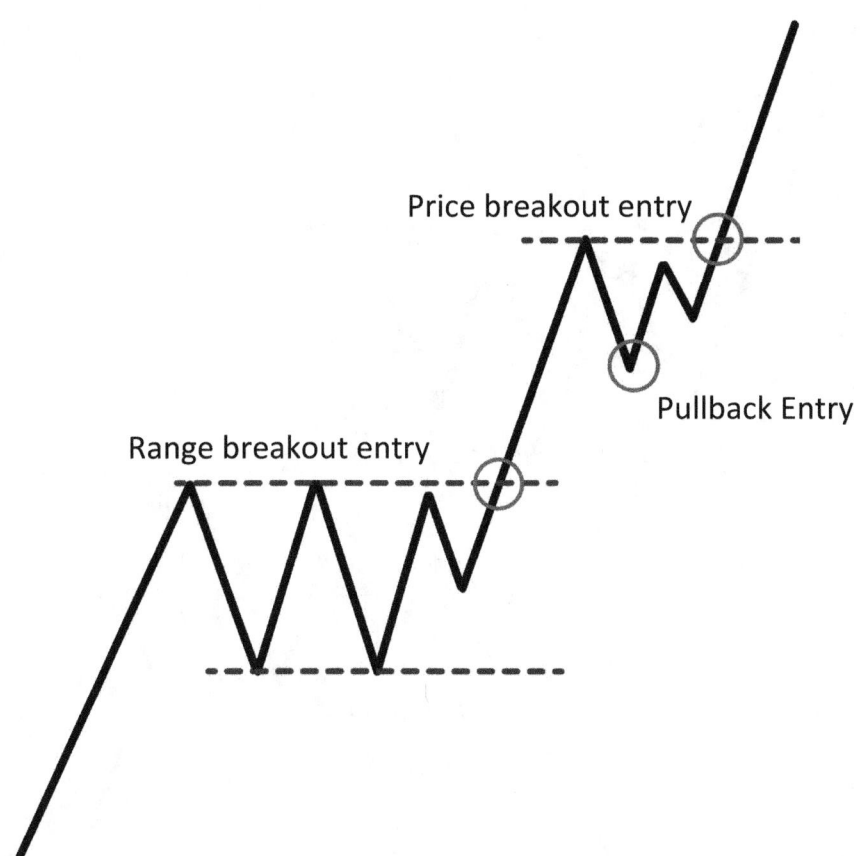

A breakout happens when a price exceeds a significant resistance level, indicating a potential trend reversal or acceleration. A subsequent pullback refers to a temporary retracement or dip before the uptrend continues, providing an opportunity for traders to buy or enter long positions.

Breakdown and Pullback

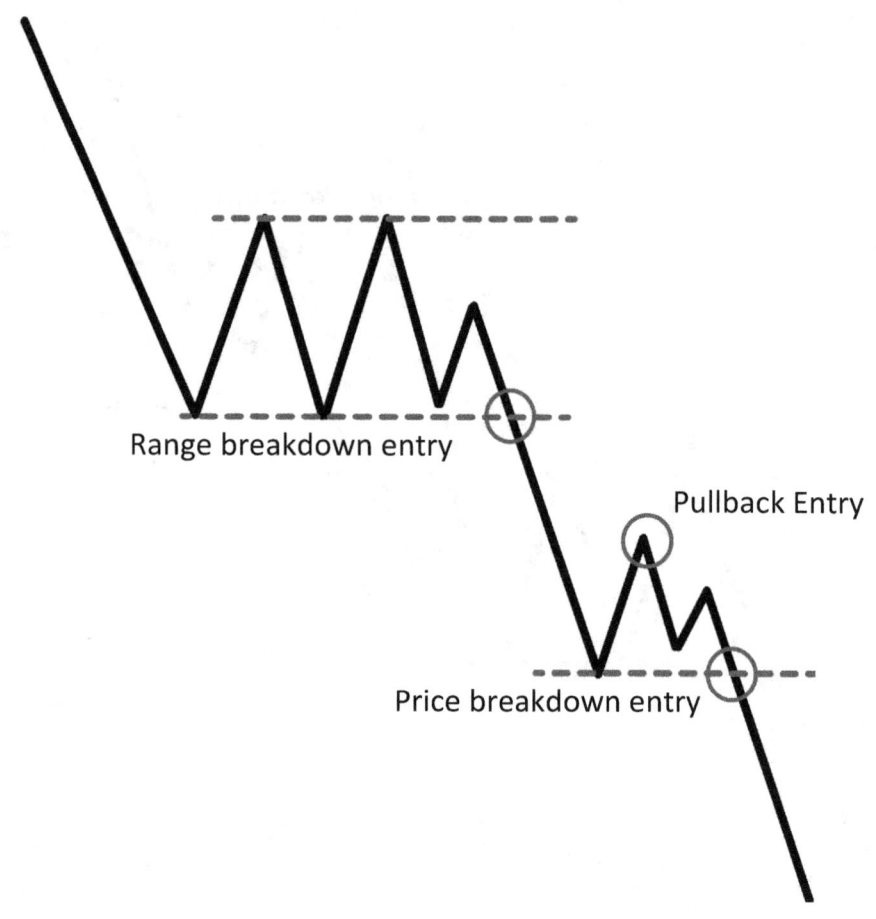

Range breakdown entry

Pullback Entry

Price breakdown entry

A breakdown refers to a price movement that falls below a significant support level, suggesting a potential trend reversal or acceleration in the downward direction. A subsequent pullback is a temporary retracement or bounce before the downtrend continues.

Volume Analysis

Volume is the number of trades that happened in a certain security during a certain time frame.

A lot of technical analysts use volume as an important factor when they look at stocks. Investors can figure out how important changes in a security's price are by looking at trends in both volume and price.

Many day traders and swing traders look at volume to figure out how strong the current trend is.

When people are new to trading or are losing money, I've noticed that they often don't look at volume. From what I know, traders will benefit from understanding volume, which will give them an edge over other traders.

If you look at the table on the next page, you can see how rising or falling volume is interpreted against rising or falling security prices.

Price → Volume		→ Significance
Rising Price	Rising Volume	Very Strong Bullish Momentum
Rising Price	Falling Volume	Unreliable Bullish Momentum
Falling Price	Rising Volume	Very Strong Bearish Momentum
Falling Price	Falling Volume	Unreliable Bearish Momentum

Most of the time, a big rise in both price and volume is seen as a reliable or very strong sign of either a continuing bullish trend or a bullish reversal. But if the price is going up but not many people are buying or selling, it is seen as unreliable.

In the same way, a big drop in price followed by a big rise in volume is often seen as a good or very strong sign of a continuing bearish trend or a bearish reversal. But if the price is going down and there aren't many orders, it's not a good sign.

Risk Management

Risk management is one of the most important parts of trading if you want to be successful, but most traders don't pay attention to it.

Believe it or not, I've seen a lot of traders and investors who don't pay much attention to risk management when trading or investing and end up losing a lot of money as a result.

"The most profitable traders don't just analyze charts; they master the art of managing risk."

Another important thing to always keep in mind is that the bigger your loss, the harder it will be to get it back in the future.

This can be seen by looking at the table on next page.

% LOSS	% GAIN REQUIRED
10	11
20	25
30	43
40	67
50	100
60	150
70	233
80	400
90	900

You need an 11% gain to recover from a 10% loss. To recover from a 50% loss, you must gain 100% in the future. Thus, trading risk must always be managed.

Risk Management

Risk management helps traders cut their loses and keeps them from losing all of their money. After all, a trader who has made a lot of money can lose it all in just one or two bad trades if they don't have a good way to handle risk.

Even though risk management is a key part of long-term success in investing, many people still don't pay enough attention to it.

So, please don't underestimate how important risk management is in your investing journey.

Position Sizing

The size of a trader's position is an important way to control risk when dealing. In fact, risk management starts before you even make a trade with the size of your account.

As the name suggests, it is a way for a trader to decide how big of a position to take when dealing. In other words, it means the amount of money a trader puts into a particular trade.

When choosing the size of a trader's position, it's important to think about how willing he is to take risks and how much money he has to trade with.

Position sizing is a way for professional traders to decide how much of an investment they should buy or sell. This helps them reduce risk and make the most money possible.

If your stock size is too big or too small, you might end up taking too much risk or not enough risk for a trade to make you enough money.

How to Figure Out Position Size -

Before we learn how to figure out what the best position size is, let's try to understand two important things about it:

1. Account Risk
2. Trade Risk

Account Risk is a set percentage of your trading capital or a particular amount that you can use to limit the amount of risk you are willing to take on each trade.

So, if you have $5000 in trading capital and have set your risk limit at 1%, you are ready to risk up to $500 per trade.

Most of the time, a trader shouldn't put more than 2% to 5% of his trading cash at risk on any one trade. Not only that, but the risk limit for the account should stay the same for all trades.

Trade Risk is the difference between where you start the deal and where you put your stop loss order.

The stop loss is set by a set of rules that I'll talk about in the next part.

So, if you bought shares of a company for $200 and set a stop loss at $190, your trade risk would be $10 per share.

Now that you know how far your stop loss is from your starting point (in dollar), you can figure out how big your trade should be.

Ideal position size = Account risk / Trade risk

For example: Consider a trader with $50,000 in trading capital who wants to buy shares of ABC Company at $90 with a stop loss of $86 and a price goal of $100.

Here's how to figure out what the trader's best dealing size should be:

If the trader sets a 2% risk cap for all trades, the account risk will be 2% of $50,000 = $1,000.

Entry - Stop Loss = $90 - $86 = $4

Now, the best size of a position is $1000/4 = 250 shares.

Let's say that ABC Company buys and sells derivatives in lots of 25 shares.

In this case, the person can either trade 250 shares on the cash market or 10 lots (250/25) in derivatives.

If you use this method, you will always end up with the best position size, no matter how the market is moving, how the trade is set up, or what strategy you are using.

So, you should never trade more than you can afford and handle emotionally. Position size is an important part of this.

Psychology of Trading

Mastering Your Mind for Market Success

We will look into the fascinating and sometimes hard-to-understand world of trading psychology. Trading isn't just about numbers and charts; it's also about controlling your emotions, staying disciplined, and sticking to your trading plan. For long-term success in the ever-changing world of financial markets, it's important to understand and use the psychological aspects of trading.

Emotions and Their Impact on Trading Decisions

Understanding the Emotional Roller Coaster

Trading is a high-risk game that constantly puts your emotional strength to the test. In this chapter, we'll learn more about the complicated link between emotions and trading decisions. By understanding this emotional roller coaster, you can make better trading decisions and do better in the market.

Emotion vs. Rationality

- **The Battle Within:** When you trade, your emotions and logic often go to war with each other. Learn how this internal struggle works and what it means for your trading decisions.
- **Impulsive vs. Thoughtful Decisions:** Emotions can lead to rash, gut-level choices, while rationality can help you make smart, logical decisions. Find a middle ground between the two.

Fear and Greed

- **The Twin Tyrants:** Fear and greed are two strong emotions that drive a lot of what happens on the market. Find out how they affect traders and investors and why they can be both an incentive and a trap.
- **Managing Fear:** How to deal with and control the paralyzing effects of fear so that it doesn't get in the way of your trading decisions when they are most important.

Taming Greed: Ways to keep greed in check and not overextend yourself or chase gains that aren't possible.

The Impact of Loss Aversion

- **The Losses Weigh More:** Loss aversion is a psychological bias that makes people feel the pain of losses more strongly than the happiness of gains of the same size. Know how this bias can affect the trades you make.
- **Mitigating Loss Aversion:** Use strategies to reduce the effects of loss aversion, such as setting predetermined stop-loss levels and rethinking losses as learning experiences.

we've talked about how emotions and logic work together in trading. Fear, greed, and not wanting to lose are all strong emotions that can either drive you to success or make you make mistakes that cost you a lot of money. By understanding how they affect you and using good techniques for dealing with your emotions, you can ride the emotional roller coaster of trading with more confidence and strength.

Dear Readers,

I wanted to take a moment to send you a short message of encouragement and motivation. Trading can be a challenging journey, filled with ups and downs, but it is also a path that holds tremendous potential for financial growth and personal fulfillment.

In the world of trading, perseverance is key. It is the ability to keep going, even in the face of obstacles, that separates successful traders from the rest. Remember, every setback is an opportunity to learn and grow. Embrace the challenges and keep pushing forward.

Continuous learning is another vital aspect of trading. The markets are constantly evolving, and staying ahead requires a commitment to expanding your knowledge and honing your skills. Seek out educational resources, attend seminars, and connect with experienced traders. The more you know, the more empowered you become.

Risk management is the cornerstone of any successful trading strategy. It is important to approach trading with a disciplined mindset and a well-defined plan. Set realistic goals, manage your risk effectively, and always prioritize the preservation of capital. By doing so, you'll be better equipped to navigate the uncertainties of the market.

Lastly, remember that trading is not a solitary endeavor. Surround yourself with a supportive community of like-minded individuals who share your passion for trading. Engage in discussions, seek advice, and learn from the experiences of others. Together, we can inspire each other to achieve greatness.

Believe in yourself and your abilities. Trust that you have what it takes to unlock your full potential as a trader. With dedication, perseverance, and a commitment to continuous learning, you can achieve your financial goals.

Wishing you all the best on your trading journey.

Warm regards,

- By Author